BIBLE STUDY COMMENTARY

# Deuteronomy

## LOUIS GOLDBERG

**Lamplighter Books** Grand Rapids, Michigan
Zondervan Publishing House

DEUTERONOMY: BIBLE STUDY COMMENTARY

Copyright © 1986 by Louis Goldberg

Lamplighter Books are published by the Zondervan Publishing House
1415 Lake Drive, S.E., Grand Rapids, Michigan 49506

**Library of Congress Cataloging in Publication Data**

Goldberg, Louis, 1923–
  Deuteronomy : Bible study commentary

  (Bible study commentary series)
  "Lamplighter books,"
  Bibliography: p.
  1. Bible. O.T. Deuteronomy—Commentaries. I. Title. II. Series.
BS1275.3.G65  1986      222'.1507      86-13333
ISBN 0-310-20201-9

*Edited by Pamela M. Hartung*

*Printed in the United States of America*

90 91 / 10 9 8 7 6 5 4 3 2

# Contents

# Preface

Deuteronomy has a greater impact on the Old and New Testaments than any other book of the Bible. For most Christians, however, the Book of Deuteronomy remains a dry and uninteresting book.

Most Christians view Deuteronomy, as well as Leviticus, as the law. When I ask believers what they mean by the phrase "the law," I find that most will reply, "Well, the books of Moses are the law, but we are now into the New Testament which emphasizes grace." Christians often are unable to deal with the tension between the law and grace. Some feel that we must shun the law because, after all, it is by grace we are saved and grace allows us to serve the living God. Other Christians are uncomfortable with the idea of grace and construct a system of "works righteousness," trying through their human effort to enter the kingdom of God. Deuteronomy helps us see the positive, creative tension between law and grace. Deuteronomy does not call for righteousness through self-effort but righteousness that comes from a circumcised heart in response to God's gracious acts.

In the Book of Deuteronomy, Moses set forth the Ten Commandments (or the Decalogue) and proceeded to expound, interpret, and apply these commandments to the second generation of Israelites who had come out of Egypt. Many Christians, however, feel uneasy when any emphasis is put on the Ten Commandments. Somehow it appears that an undue interest in this part of the law does not coincide with the law of love one lives by when knowing Christ. But herein lies a problem. How can one talk about the love of Christ without realizing that the highest love, *hesed* (Old Testament) and *agape* (New Testament), cannot be divorced from the ethics of the commandments undergirded by the righteousness and holiness of God? In any born-again experience, whether in an Old or New Testament experience, the law is written on the heart. And the main component of the law is the commandments. Christians need an ethic to guide them. God's people, therefore, need to be exposed to the commandments and their interpretations found in the Book of Deuteronomy.

The document of Deuteronomy is not a dry and dusty book, presented only to the Israelites. Many of its lessons have vital modern-day applications. Today's Christians can read Deuteronomy and 1) discover a faith-life that is captured by God's love and that responds by serving Him; 2) know that the God of the universe can lead in their life, enabling them to conquer today's giants who oppose the believer's outreach; 3) find guidelines for godly service by civil authorities; 4) find encouragement for the preservation of the family and instructions for child training; 5) find guidelines to curb immorality and divorce; 6) find instructions for forgiveness of loans; and 7) find warnings against taking away the rights of the poor, downtrodden, widows, and orphans.

Finally, Deuteronomy warns that while the Lord is a compassionate and loving God, He is not a "granddaddy in the sky" who finds it difficult to act in judgment when deplorable moral issues require Him to do so. He is righteous and can step in to curb evil among nations as well as in individuals. He is not powerless to act when situations warrant it.

If we study the Book of Deuteronomy with an open mind and heart, we will find the basis for ethical behavior and realize that it can drastically change our lives. The early Jewish believers knew this book well, and it became a part of their lifestyle and preaching. I trust that you, likewise, can have a fresh experience with the living God as Deuteronomy becomes a part of your mindset and walk with the Lord.

# Acknowledgments

I have deep respect for the teachers who have contributed greatly to my heritage as a Jewish lad. I also pay tribute to Dr. Arnold Schultz of Northern Baptist Theological Seminary, under whom I was privileged to sit. His expertise in exegeting the Hebrew Scriptures (Old Testament) was of great value to me.

Through the years as I have taught Studies in the Pentateuch (the Torah) to eager students, I have come to realize that the students have been among my best teachers. I wish to express my sincerest appreciation to Laurel Coker, who typed the first draft, and to both Laurel Coker and Pam Rather, who typed the final copy. Most important, I express deep thankfulness to God for the loving help and encouragement of a dear wife who has served with me in the ministry.

# Introduction

The Book of Genesis describes how God called Abraham and established through him the family that eventually became the people of Israel.

The Book of Exodus describes Israel's liberation from slavery in Egypt and her establishment as a people at Mount Sinai. There a covenant was sealed between Israel and God, with Moses serving as the mediator. The covenant spelled out the terms of a theocracy, and from the vantage point of Sinai, the Israelites still looked forward to having a land that they could call their own.

The Book of Leviticus instructs the people of Israel in the worship of their God-King. The specifications for the sacrifices were provided to teach a people how they could know the Lord and yield their lives to Him in total dedication. God's instructions included 1) how the priests and Levites were to be dedicated and function as His servants; 2) how a nation should discern what was good for food; 3) how people were to care for themselves, keeping diseases at a minimum; 4) how people were to practice a moral code that reflected the holiness and righteousness of the true and living God; 5) how a nation was to be governed through the juridical (legal) system or its civil and criminal law codes; 6) how people could give praise to God and thank Him through specific holidays; 7) how people were to pay careful attention to their relationship with God or suffer dire consequences; and finally, 8) how a nation was to honor its God through tithes and offerings.[1]

The Book of Numbers, in narrative form, describes how the people of Israel moved from Mount Sinai to Kadesh-Barnea, the point from which they were to enter the Land of Promise. Tragically, the first generation failed in their attempt and were made to wander for thirty-eight years in the wilderness, until every one perished except Caleb and Joshua. The Book of Numbers concludes with second generation Israelites encamped in the plains of Moab, opposite Jericho. Once more they were on the threshold of entering the land of promise (Num. 33:48–49; Deut. 1:5).

In the Book of Deuteronomy, Moses reminds the second Israelite generation of their previous experiences in the Sinai as well as of their parents' failures. He reminds them that God did not make a mistake in forcing them to wait. Rather, He wanted His people to remember their responsibility to Him, their King, and to love Him with all their heart, soul, and strength (6:5). By no means, however, was this a message only for Israel; we are reminded that believers today are to honor the Lord in the same way.

Deuteronomy is one of the greatest pieces of literature in the Old Testament. It influenced not only Israel but the New Testament as well. There are over eighty citations of Deuteronomy in all but six books of the New Testament (John, Col., 1 Thess., 2 Tim., and 1 and 2 Peter). During His temptation by Satan in the wilderness, Jesus quoted from this book three times (Deut. 8:3; 6:13, 16). The early Jewish Christians frequently quoted from it as well.

## Title

The Book of Deuteronomy has been known to Jewish people by a number of names: 1) *Elleh Haddebarim*—"These are the words," (Jewish people usually designate the titles of their books by the first word or words of the book itself); 2) *Debarim*—"words"; 3) *Mishneh Hattorah*—"the law, a second time"; and 4) *Sefer Takahot*—"book of admonitions."

[1] Louis Goldberg, *Bible Study Commentary: Leviticus* (Grand Rapids: Zondervan Publishing House, 1980).

The title *Deuteronomy* literally means "second law" and is derived from the Greek (Septuagint) translation of 17:18 which was misunderstood: the phrase "a copy of this law" was translated as "this second" or "repeated law." Once established in Greek, the title remained fixed, and the Latin Vulgate translated it as Deuteronomium, a second law. While God had already ratified this law with Israel and while Moses had expanded on it in Deuteronomy, the title is not entirely inaccurate.

With this book as part of the Old Testament Canon, Israel's leaders recognized early that Deuteronomy was a fundamental part of the sacred writings. Already in the first century A.D., the book was widely accepted and authoritative for Israel because of the many quotations from it in the New Testament. In addition, Deuteronomy was one of the most widely used books in the sectarian literature of Qumran.[2] These people, largely a nonconformist group within Israel, never forgot the covenant drawn up at Sinai between God and Israel. Neither did they forget its renewal on the plains of Moab by a second generation.[3]

Close parallels exist between the Middle Eastern treaties in the second millennium B.C. and Deuteronomy. We, therefore, can surmise that the events recorded in Deuteronomy occurred in the same period as the Middle Eastern treaties. Meredith Kline has stated: "The beginnings of canonical Scripture thus coincided with the formal founding of Israel as the kingdom of God. In the treaty documents given by our Lord, at the very origins of the nation Israel, the people of God already possessed the ground stratum of the Old Testament canon."[4]

## Deuteronomy: The Torah

Deuteronomy describes itself as "law" or "Torah." Torah basically means "divine instruction," an emphasis which is repeated in the phrases "this Book of the Law" (28:61; 29:21; 30:10; 31:26) and "this law" (1:5; 4:8; 17:18, 19; 27:3, 8, 26).

---

[2] Also known as the Dead Sea Scroll Community.

[3] See Peter C. Craigie, *Deuteronomy*, in *The New International Commentary on the Old Testament* (Grand Rapids: Wm. B. Eerdmans Publishing Company, 1976), pp. 84–86 for a detailed concordance of principal Qumran manuscripts relating to Deuteronomy.

[4] Meredith G. Kline, *The Structure of Biblical Authority* (Grand Rapids: Wm. B. Eerdmans Publishing Company, 1972), p. 38.

Besides the specific use of Torah, a number of other derivatives of this term appear in the text: 1) "stipulations" or "testimonies" (NASV) from the Hebrew *'edut*, meaning "solemn charges"; 2) "decrees" or "statutes" (NASV) from the Hebrew *hakkin*, meaning "what is prescribed and expected for obedience"; and 3) "laws," "ordinances" (NASV), "judgments" (AV)—all three in 4:45—from the Hebrew *mishpatim*, meaning "decisions." At times, two of the terms will appear side by side, "stipulations and decrees" (6:17) or "decrees and laws" (4:1).

These terms could have legal connotations, but since Deuteronomy is a book of the Torah, the terms refer to the divine instruction taught by Israel's priests, prophets, and sages (the wise men). Even though kings and judges may have needed Deuteronomy to help them administer the law in civil or criminal cases, the Book of Deuteronomy was never given for this reason alone. God also provided His instruction to teach the Israelites how to have atonement for their sins and how to live godly lives.

Too often Christians regard the law merely as a set of legalisms, and they view Jewish people as trying to follow the letter of the law. On the other hand, these very Christians will then proclaim that the new covenant describes how God works in grace to redeem His people and shower His love on them. In no way should such a compartmentalization exist between Old and New Testaments. Indeed, Deuteronomy itself describes how God blessed Israel and shared His love with them because of His grace and mercy. What the Lord expected from Israel in return was an outpouring of love. While some people misappropriated God's intentions and developed a legalistic substitute, a remnant in every generation always deeply loved, honored, and served the Lord their God.

### Structure

Traditionally, Deuteronomy has been accepted as a unified literary piece written by Moses. But several Jewish scholars in the Middle Ages, particularly Spinoza (1632–1637) in his *Tractatus Theologico Politicus VIII*, "The Authorship of the Pentateuch," suggested that the book did not become a finished product until the seventh century B.C. Critics in the church drew

on this suggestion. Within the last one hundred years these
critics have used form and redaction criticism to analyze the
component parts as well as the internal textual material of
Deuteronomy. Many critics have concluded that Deuteronomy
appeared in 621 B.C.[5] In form criticism, the "basic assumption is
that the earlier oral use of the tradition shaped the material and
resulted in the variety of literary forms found in the final written
record."[6] The form critic assesses Deuteronomy by its earlier
oral materials; the remainder of the book was added over the
centuries. In redaction criticism, the primary focus is on the
theological concerns of the writer as distinguished from earlier
materials. Deuteronomy focuses not on the theological concerns
of those who produced this book in 621 B.C., but on the strands of
oral materials of an earlier period. Whether these critics use
form or redaction criticism to analyze the strands behind the
present form of the book, their claim is that it was not written in
the days of Moses.

Not all scholars in the past hundred years have given up on
the unity of Deuteronomy. E. W. Nicholson has provided a list
of scholars who hold out for the unity of Deuteronomy.[7] Some of
the more prominent ones are Meredith Kline's *Treaty of the
Great King*; G. T. Manley's *The Book of the Law: Studies in the
Date of Deuteronomy*; M. H. Segal's "The Composition of the
Pentateuch—A Fresh Examination"; and E. J. Young's *An
Introduction to the Old Testament*. The weight of these
scholars for setting Deuteronomy in the early date has been
minimal in light of criticism that insists that the book appeared
at a much later date.

Since the mid-1950s, however, scholars have taken a fresh
approach to the structure of Deuteronomy. Because of their
studies of the Middle Eastern vassal or suzerainty treaties
(treaties between the overlord and his subjects), scholars have
noted a striking similarity between the Middle Eastern treaties

---

[5]See Gerhard von Rad, *Deuteronomy*, trans. Dorothea Barton (Philadelphia:
Westminster Press, 1966), who handles Deuteronomy from the form criticism
position.

[6]Floyd V. Filson, "Form Criticism," in *Twentieth Century Encyclopedia of
Religious Knowledge*, ed. Lefferts A. Loetscher (Grand Rapids: Baker Book
House, 1955), p. 436.

[7]E. W. Nicholson, *Deuteronomy and Tradition* (Philadelphia: Fortress Press,
1967) p. 37, n.1.

and the Hebrew covenant in Deuteronomy. G. E. Mendenhall demonstrated similarities between the Hittite treaties of the second millennium B.C. and the covenant between Israel and the Lord.[8] He suggests that each treaty contained several key elements:

1. The preamble, introducing the king.
2. The historical prologue, providing both a history of the events leading to the treaty and the treaty's purpose.
3. General and specific stipulations of the treaty.
4. Curses and blessings of the treaty.
5. Witnesses (various deities) who guarantee the agreement.

Mendenhall includes a sixth element that described where the document of the treaty was to be held for safekeeping as well as for its occasional public reading.

Meredith Kline, who also insists that Deuteronomy is a unity, suggests that the covenant is set in the cultural pattern of the typical Middle Eastern treaty even though Moses structured the covenant to reflect a special agreement between God and Israel. Kline arranges Deuteronomy with the following elements:

1. Preamble: the covenant mediator (1:1–5)
2. The historical prologue: covenant history (1:6–4:49)
3. Stipulations: covenant life
   a. The great commandment (5:1–11:32)
   b. Ancillary commandments (12:1–26:19)
4. Sanctions: covenant ratification, blessings and curses, covenant oath, restoration, decision (27:1–30:20)
5. Dynastic disposition: covenant continuity (31:1–34:12)[9]

Two other scholars observed a similar arrangement: D. J. McCarthy[10] as well as G. J. Wenham.[11] The latter sees the

---

[8] G. E. Mendenhall, in his "Ancient Oriental and Biblical Law," *Biblical Archaeologist*, (May, 1954), pp. 50–67 and his "Covenant Forms in Israelite Tradition," *Biblical Archaeologist*, (Sept., 1954), pp. 26–46.

[9] Kline, *Treaty of the Great King*, pp. 9–10.

[10] D. J. McCarthy, *Treaty and Covenant* (Rome: Pontifical Biblical Institute, 1963), pp. 131ff.

[11] G. J. Wenham, *The Structure and Date of Deuteronomy* (unpublished thesis), pp. 210–13 cited by J. A. Thompson, *Deuteronomy* in *The Tyndale Old Testament Commentaries* (Downers Grove, IL: InterVarsity, 1974), p. 23.

covenant form of Deuteronomy (which can also be detected in Exod. 20; Josh. 24; 1 Sam. 12) as a distinctive arrangement, although because of similar cultural patterns of the Middle East in the second millennium B.C., we would expect to find some resemblance to the law codes and treaties of this period:

| Hammurabi Law Code | O.T. Covenant | Middle Eastern Treaty |
|---|---|---|
| | | 1. Preamble |
| 1. Prologue | 1. Historical prologue | 2. Historical prologue |
| 2. Laws | 2. Stipulations | 3. Stipulations |
| | a) basic | a) basic |
| | b) detailed | b) detailed |
| 3. Summary/ Document clause | 3. Document clause | 4. Document clause |
| 4. Blessing | 4. Blessing | 5. God list |
| 5. Curse | 5. Curse | 6. Curses and |
| | 6. Recapitulation | blessings |

The mention of recapitulation under Old Testament covenant is peculiar to this covenant.

J. A. Thompson suggests an Old Testament covenant form for Deuteronomy chapters 1–30, with some slight modification (leaving off some of the Middle Eastern treaty editorial headings).[12]

| | |
|---|---|
| 1:6–3:29 | Historical prologue |
| 4:1–40; 5:1–11:32 | Basic stipulations |
| 12:1–26:19 | Detailed stipulations |
| 27:1–26 | Document clause |
| 28:1–14 | Blessings |
| 28:15–68 | Curses |
| 29:1–30:20 | Recapitulation |

Thompson also points out that chapters 31–34 are not actually a part of the form of the covenant, but rather they emphasize a covenant renewal. Joshua is mentioned in these chapters. He was chosen as Moses' successor to serve as Israel's tactical general under God's leadership. He also was given the task of dividing the land among the tribes (31:2–8). Moses' song mentions a number of elements of the covenant (32:1–43), and

---

[12]Thompson, *Deuteronomy*, p. 19.

his blessing of the tribes is linked to the Land of Promise (chap. 33). Even as Moses viewed the land from Mount Pisgah (34:1ff.), he still echoed the theme of the blessings of 33:6–28. These chapters also mention that as each future leader comes on the scene, the covenant between God and His people is to be renewed, and the people are charged with the responsibility to follow the Lord and respond to His love and grace.

## Theology

Once we recognize the Book of Deuteronomy in the form of a treaty between God and Israel, it is possible to ascertain some of the great theological ideas. Israel's God was the King. He is also regarded as the Lord, the Judge, and the General of Israel's armies. Israel, then, is the servant of the King, with responsibilities to listen and serve Him.

### The Preamble

In the Hittite suzerainty treaties, the opening statements emphasized the words spoken by the Hittite king. In the same way, Deuteronomy begins: "These are the words that Moses spoke to all Israel . . ." (1:1). While there are similarities between Deuteronomy and the Hittite document, there are also some very important differences. Although the words that Moses speaks are his, they are more importantly God's words. Moses is the spokesperson for God, Israel's king.

The term "king" designating the Lord does not often appear in the Old Testament (although, see 33:5). Perhaps the Lord did not want this term confused with the small city-state kings who served their pagan gods and goddesses. Therefore, the Lord chose other ways of expressing His royalty: "To the Lord your God belong the heavens, even the highest heavens" (10:14); and ". . . The Lord your God is God of gods and Lord of lords, the great God, mighty and awesome" (10:17). (See also 4:35; 6:4.)

Moses, God's spokesperson, was a unique prophet: "Since then, no prophet has risen in Israel like Moses, whom the Lord knew face to face" (34:10). As a prophet, he spoke the words of God (1:6). But he also interpreted and applied God's words to Israel's needs and outlined Israel's goals and objectives. It is no wonder that Jewish people to this day regard him as "Moses, our teacher."

## Historical Prologue

Middle Eastern treaties began with a historical prologue, which first described the past relationships between the king and his vassals and then outlined the future association between the overlord and his subject-leader. The treaty expressed the king's kindness to his vassals; the latter had to be responsible to the wishes of the former.

We see this form in the historical prologue to Deuteronomy. Moses recalls God's kindness and favor to Abraham, to the patriarchs (1:8), to Israel in the great redemption from Egypt, in the giving of the law at Mount Horeb, in forgiving Israel in spite of her failure at Kadesh-Barnea, and in bringing a second generation to the plains of Moab. The historical prologue traces the Lord's great acts of redemption and deliverance (chapters 1–3). God appealed to Israel to accept the treaty, with Him as the overlord. Once they did, they were to be faithful to Him, a theme that occurs throughout Deuteronomy. In future renewals of the covenant, successive generations also were called on to be faithful to their king.

In the Middle Eastern treaties, the suzerain (king or overlord) promised to protect his subjects from their enemies and to go to war against those enemies who refused to acknowledge his sovereignty over his people. Similarly, in Deuteronomy, the Lord promises to lead His people to the Promised Land and to protect them in their battles with their enemies. God would not only lead them against their physical enemies, but against their spiritual enemies as well. God, the Lord, who opposed the gods and goddesses of His enemies in the land of promise, asked His people to destroy the pagan worship system. He did not brook any rivals; neither was Israel to provoke Him by being involved with any false worship.

## Basic Stipulations

The Middle Eastern treaties gave general stipulations for the future relationships between the two parties drawing up the treaty. In Deuteronomy's treaty, the Lord stipulated that Israel was to be the subject-vassal to Him, the universal Suzerain. Because of His sovereign will, He chose Israel. He did not choose the Israelites because they had something special or

distinctive to their credit; they were the fewest of all peoples
(7:6–8). Once chosen, Israel became "his treasured possession"
or *segullah* (26:18). God's special care is reflected in the way He
redeemed Israel from slavery. The word *redeem* (*padah*), as
used in other Semitic languages, meant "to free someone who
was in servitude to another by paying a ransom" (see 7:8; 9:26;
15:15; and 24:18), and it aptly described Israel's redemption. In
21:8, the word has a more general application. Another more
basic word, *to save* (*hoshi'ah*), is also used (20:4; 33:29). In
response, Israel was to set herself apart to the Lord.

A second general stipulation was love. The Lord set His
affection on Israel and took the initiative to shower His love on
His people (7:7–8) by entering into a covenant with them and
giving them His commandments (5:6–21). And, because of His
love for them, He would take the pains to discipline them like a
caring father; the Lord promised to be faithful to a thousand
generations, but they in turn were to love Him (7:9).

Another basic stipulation was that love would need to be
tangibly expressed. Israel would express love to her king in a
number of ways: 1) Israel was to walk in His ways (8:6; 10:12;
etc.); 2) Israel was to fear and revere Him (4:10; 6:2, 13, 24, etc.);
3) the nation was to hold fast to the Lord (4:4; 10:20; etc.); and
finally, 4) the people were to serve Him (6:13; 10:12, 20, etc.).

It is important to recognize that these basic stipulations
were addressed not only to the nation but also to every
individual within the nation. Every Israelite was to feel that the
covenant had been made with him or her personally, and each
person was to respond accordingly. Furthermore, no person was
expected to live these basic stipulations in order to earn favor
with God through some legalistic observance. Israel's holiness
was not attainable by works righteousness; instead, God set the
nation aside and called on individuals to respond in love to His
revelation, to find an atonement for their sin, and to thereby live
a life expressive of His holiness.

### Detailed Stipulations

Deuteronomy 12–26 lists many detailed stipulations for
Israel's relationship to her Lord. These laws cover worship, the
sanctuary, idolatry, religious festivals, conduct of war, immoral-

ity, dietary codes, duties of officials (including judges, kings, priests, and prophets), inheritance, theft, false witnesses, and even the treatment of wild animals. Every aspect of life is covered—the ceremonial, moral, civil, and criminal law as well as the model of worship and lifestyle. At the same time, warnings were issued against the pagan practices of the Canaanite people, including severe penalties for being involved with them.

Israel was like a household. The Lord called on each person to guard his or her own conduct, which would have repercussions on the nation at large. The community had a responsibility for every person among them. A person's love for the community was to extend to neighbors, aliens, the poor and underprivileged—even the animals. A person's love for others reflected his or her love for God. The connection was not to be taken lightly; a person's love for God was expressed by what he or she did in following the stipulations.

Another aspect of Israel's relationship to the Lord was to remember continually what He did for His people. The theme of deliverance from Egypt was to be remembered every year at the Feast of Unleavened Bread. The act of remembrance was not an exercise limited to only one generation; instead, every generation was to remember this deliverance as a part of Israel's living history. When God's people remember how He acted in love and compassion, they respond to Him in love.

*Blessings and Curses*

The Deuteronomic treaty also included blessings and curses. The emphasis on blessings and curses was a reminder that as Israel was responsive to the Lord, He would then shower them with His blessings—a long life and a continued presence in the Land of Promise. The curses served as a discipline; the worst judgment was for the nation to suffer exile, which, however, was never to be permanent. Deuteronomy mentions more curses than blessings to underscore God's warning that if people became disobedient, He would act in judgment to preserve a faithful remnant.

God's blessings for His people meant He was in control not only of history but also of nature, providing food in abundance, controlling disease, making the land fruitful, and causing nations to fear Israel, thereby giving His people peace and rest. But if Israel chose to snub the Lord of the covenant and to worship other gods and goddesses, then the sovereign Lord could also bring destruction on the land and cause nations to attack them.

Tragically, while the second generation willingly promised to live by the stipulations of the covenant, certain succeeding generations were not faithful at all, despite God's warnings through the prophets. Subsequently, He sent them into exile twice, once to Babylon in the fifth century B.C. and then on a world-wide dispersion since the first century. While God's judgment dealt with sin, it was also active in restoration. Many times His discipline preserved a remnant of people who would respond to His love.

When Paul cited Deuteronomy 27:26 (in Gal. 3:10), "Cursed is everyone who does not continue to do everything written in the Book of the Law," he reminded us that we do not gain God's favor through works of righteousness. Even as Israel was to respond to God's love, so we are to respond to His love in Christ and receive a new life. Once we have a new relationship with God, we are enabled to live a righteous life. In both the Old and New Testaments, God never called on people to follow His commandments legalistically.[13]

## Date and Authorship

Until the Middle Ages, neither Judaism nor Christianity questioned Moses' authorship of Deuteronomy; both also agreed that the entire book was written by Moses. While some early Jewish scholars have questioned the traditional view,[14] it was not until the late eighteenth and early nineteenth centuries that modern critical scholars asserted that Moses did not write Deuteronomy. Instead, they attributed Deuteronomy to other writers who lived at a later date—either Samuel in the eleventh

---

[13] For a select bibliography on the theology of Deuteronomy see Craigie, *Deuteronomy*, p. 45.

[14] R. K. Harrison, *Introduction to Old Testament* (Grand Rapids: Wm. B. Eerdmans Publishing Company, 1969), pp. 3–18.

century B.C. or religious leaders during the seventh century B.C. and even possibly in the post-exilic period.[15]

Because the conservative viewpoint of date and authorship since the 1950s is based on a study of the similarities between the structure of Deuteronomy and the Middle Eastern suzerainty treaties, the claim is that Deuteronomy should be dated in the Mosaic period.[16] Kline has suggested that Deuteronomy "is a covenant renewal document, which in its total structure exhibits the classical legal form of the suzerainty treaties of the Mosaic age."[17] Kline contends that when one recognizes that a biblical document reflects the historical and cultural background of a specific period, it is reasonable to date it where it harmonizes best, rather than date it in a period where it will be an anachronism (out of harmony) with the age in which it is purported to be written.

Other scholars, like M. Weinfeld, have disagreed.[18] Weinfeld dates Deuteronomy in the seventh century B.C., claiming that its structure is more akin to the Esarhaddon Assyrian state treaties of this period. He contends that Deuteronomy's curses are longer and more elaborate than the earlier Hittite treaties' curses, which tend to be short and generalized. Concerning Weinfeld's thesis, Craigie asks whether "there is a clear distinction and form between the treaty patterns of the second millennium and that of the first millennium B.C."[19] Those who insist a difference exists point to the Hittite treaties which have an historical prologue, while the first millennium B.C. ones do not. Weinfeld feels that this does not constitute a strong argument against his position but suggests that perhaps some of

---

[15] For a discussion of scholars' views and arguments, see Thompson, *Deuteronomy*, pp. 49–68. Thompson's conclusion is that it is difficult to assess a date for the book, although he does insist that "Moses himself provided Israel with the heart of Deuteronomy," but that there could have been some editorial work. He dates the book at about 1100 B.C. (p. 68).

[16] K. A. Kitchen, *Ancient Orient and Old Testament* (Downers Grove, IL: InterVarsity Press, 1966), pp. 90–102; Kline, *Treaty of the Great King*, p. 8ff.; K. A. Kitchen, "Ancient Orient 'Deuteronomism' and the Old Testament," *New Perspectives on the Old Testament*, J. Barton Payne, ed. (San Diego: Harcourt, 1979), pp. 1–24.

[17] Kline, *Treaty of the Great King*, p. 28.

[18] M. Weinfeld, *Deuteronomy and the Deuteronomic School* (Oxford: Clarendon Press, 1972).

[19] Craigie, *Deuteronomy*, p. 26.

the first millennium treaties once had a prologue, but they were either lost or twisted. He also felt that historical prologues were not consistent with the mind-set of the Assyrian kings who felt they did not have to provide any reason for their actions in their treaties.

Kitchen suggests four major differences between the second and first millennium treaties: 1) in the second millennium treaties, the divine witnesses invariably appear between the stipulations and curses, which is not the case in the first millennium treaties; 2) the historical prologues differ (already discussed); 3) the second millennium treaty form includes the blessings in balance with the curses, while in the later texts there are no corresponding blessings to the curses; and 4) the form of the earlier treaties has a more consistent order than that of the first millennium treaties.[20]

Craigie raises a note of caution, however, in dating Deuteronomy in the Mosaic period, indicating that further archaeological research and discovery might not support the early dating.[21] Nevertheless, he suggests that because the book closely parallels the suzerainty treaties of the second millenium, there are good grounds today for assessing the date of Deuteronomy in the Mosaic period rather than in a later one.

To place Deuteronomy at any time other than the Mosaic period would pose problems and make the book out of sequence with its own cultural background. Although Moses was well aware of the treaty form of his day, he may have adapted it rather than copied it. While Israel was to be a vassal state, she was unlike her neighbors because her loyalty was to the Lord and to Him alone.

Another possibility of asserting a Mosaic authorship of Deuteronomy is to examine very carefully the known historical background conditions and do a careful literary analysis of the book. The research by G. T. Manley has demonstrated that the Deuteronomy text itself can be placed only in a period near the conquest under Joshua.[22]

---

[20] Kitchen, *Ancient Orient and the Old Testament*, p. 95ff.

[21] Craigie, *Deuteronomy*, pp. 27–28.

[22] Manley, *The Book of the Law*, who in his epilogue has declared, ". . . this treatment leads to the conclusion that the law really proceeded from and was written by Moses."

Gleason Archer argues against post-Mosaic authorship by examining two particular phrases that have been so-called "proofs" of later authorship.[23] The first phrase is, "as he is today" (2:30 NASV). The argument is that a long period of time had occurred since the days of Moses, thereby suggesting a later date and author. Archer suggests that this interpretation is arbitrary. Israel's leader was looking back at some forty years in the desert. It would have been appropriate for Moses to add this phrase expressing that all of the events of his long ministry have continued until the closing year of his life.

Archer also points out a second phrase, "east of the Jordan" in 1:1. The argument against the Mosaic authorship is that if Moses had composed the book in Moab, then the phrase "on the other side of the Jordan" could only have referred to Canaan. Therefore, the reference in 1:1 to the territories east of the Jordan River must mean that the author of Deuteronomy lived in Judah or Israel, west of the Jordan. It is true that on a number of occasions, the territory on the east side of the Jordan is referred to as "the other side of the Jordan," and in New Testament times, the lower part of this area, "Perea," was "the other-side land," no matter where a person lived. Nevertheless, if one examines the context of the passages in 3:20, 3:25, and 11:30, the phrase obviously refers to the territory west of the Jordan. Therefore, it appears that the literal and obvious sense is to be preferred rather than to make this phrase fit some arbitrary piece of geography to sustain a critical idea about who the author was and when the author lived.

Based on Deuteronomy's form and religious make-up, we will assume that it was written during Moses' time, either from his pen or from that of a scribe who lived during Moses' lifetime or shortly after his death. Even if a scribe put Deuteronomy in its final form, the major part of the book is from Moses himself (except chapter 34, which is an account of his death). The last chapter could have been written by Joshua or some scribe as an epilogue.

Moses' name appears in the first person (1:16, 18; 3:21; 29:5). The book describes events that cover about two months

---

[23]Gleason L. Archer, *A Survey of Old Testament Introduction* (Chicago: Moody Press, 1964), pp. 243–44.

(1:3; 34:5, 8; Josh. 4:19), but the review of Israel's wandering in the desert cover some thirty-eight years. The book is therefore set at about 1400 B.C., in the lifetime of Moses.

## Purpose and Theme

By the time the second generation had arrived at the east bank and was poised to enter the Land of Promise, only two first-generation people besides Moses were left—Caleb and Joshua. A second generation was now in place (2:14–16). Moses rehearses the law with them, expanding on what was given at Sinai, and tries to prepare them for entrance, conquest, and possession of Canaan.

## Most Important Words

The most important key words used in the Book of Deuteronomy include the following:

1. *Covenant* is used 27 times.
   Israel was instructed to *keep, observe, follow, obey* the commands, decrees, laws, and requirements (4:2, 40; 5:10, 29; 6:2, 17; 7:9, 11, 12; 8:2, 6, 11; 10:13; 11:1, 8, 22; 13:4, 18; 17:19; 19:9; 26:16; see also 27:1; 28:9, 45; used a total of 24 times).
2. *Love* is used 20 times.
   a. The Lord loves His people: 7 times
   b. The people love the Lord: 11 times
   c. Love for the alien: 2 times
3. *Revere* is used 19 times.
   a. Revere the Lord: 10 times
   b. Learn to revere the Lord: 5 times
   c. Revere the Lord as long as you (they) live: 4 times
4. *Listen* and *Obey* (where *obey* comes from the same verbs as *listen*) are used 18 times.
5. *Remember* (or *memory)* is used 15 times.
6. *Walk in the way(s) of the Lord* and *follow the Lord* are used 10 times.
7. *Hear, O Israel* or *Listen, O Israel* are used 6 times.
8. *Serve the Lord* is used 6 times (6:13; 10:12, 20; 11:13; 13:4; 28:47).
9. *Hold fast to the Lord* is used 5 times (4:4; 10:20; 11:22; 13:4; 30:20).

A strong tie exists between these important words and the language of the Middle Eastern treaties, thereby marking the link between the form of Deuteronomy and the treaty patterns of its own historical and cultural background.

Other phrases are important and peculiar to Deuteronomy—words that: 1) describe the foreign gods and what makes them detestable to the Lord; 2) describe the worship places where God places His name; 3) tell of the Exodus and God's mighty deliverance of Israel; 4) pertain to the Promised Land and its conquest; 5) promised blessings because of Israel's loyalty to the covenant.

So powerful was the influence of Deuteronomy on successive writers, that many of its phrases occur in the historical books from Joshua to 2 Kings as well as in Jeremiah. Later historians and prophets repeatedly referred to the renewal of the covenant in specific situations in Israel's history, and the language of Deuteronomy was very much a part of their terminology as they spoke to their particular generation. The prophets derived a certain authority in their preaching as they depended on what Moses had proclaimed.

## Preamble of the Covenant: Moses' Opening Words (1:1–5)

Moses' first words, which serve as an introduction to the book, mirror the preambles in the Middle Eastern suzerainty treaties. God ratified the covenant with His people at Sinai, and it was now to be renewed as Moses teaches the second generation of Israelites.

In accordance with the covenant, the content of Deuteronomy is presented not merely as a historical record but as Moses' spoken words. The book is an exposition of what God had given at Horeb and what Moses proclaims to the people (1:3). On only a few occasions do we see God speaking in the first person (7:4; 11:13–15; 17:3; 29:6). Moses functions as the mediator as he brings God's Word to the people.

The words are addressed to "all Israel" in the first and last verses of Deuteronomy and other passages (1:1; 5:1; 11:6; 13:11; 18:6; 21:21; 27:9; 29:1; 31:1, 7, 11; 32:45; and 34:12); "all Israel" was important to the concept of the covenant because it included all the people. The covenant relationship is not to any one specific generation, but to all Israel in every generation. God had made the covenant not only with the first generation at Sinai on the east bank of the Jordan but also with Israel yet to come.

Moses described the locale: "in the desert east of the Jordan" (1:1). The point of reference can either be the east bank as one views it from the west bank or the general area designated trans-Jordan, the area around the River Jordan.[24] The term "Arabah" refers to the Jordan Rift, the great rift of the valley which begins north of the Sea of Galilee. It seems that Moses delivered his messages from an area just north of the Dead Sea.[25]

Moses explains further that it took eleven days to go from Horeb to Kadesh-Barnea (1:2). Horeb seems to be the general term for the area of Mount Sinai and is widely used, except in 33:2. We know from modern travel that the road between Horeb and Kadesh-Barnea, called the Mount Seir road, is an eleven-day journey.[26]

Moses most likely intends to point out a contrast here. It took the first generation only eleven days to go from Mount Horeb to Kadesh-Barnea, but Moses proclaims his messages to a second generation in the fortieth year, the first day of the eleventh month (1:2–3). The first generation had rebelled against God's promises, delaying Israel's entrance into the land for forty years after the Exodus from Egypt. Moses had to patiently wait until a second generation was ready to enter the Promised Land, this time from Jordan's east bank. This verse contains the only date in the entire book, as if to mark the time when Moses began to teach the second generation, preparing them for their future experiences.

A further contrast is seen between the rebellious first generation and a faithful Moses, who continues to proclaim the divine revelation to the Israelites. What God desires is obedience, and Moses lived this obedience as an example to the people.

The writer gives further historical orientation in verse 4:

---

[24] Harrison, *Introduction to the Old Testament*, p. 637ff.
[25] Ibid.
[26] Y. Aharoni and M. Avi-Yonah, *The Macmillan Bible Atlas* (New York: The Macmillan Company, 1968), map 48.

Moses delivers his speech after he had defeated the kings of the Amorites (which is described in greater detail in 2:26–37 and 3:1–22). The reference to the Amorites is verified in the Egyptian Execration Texts, as early as about 1900 B.C.[27]

The final verse of the preamble refers again to the locale— "east of the Jordan in the territory of Moab" (1:5). Here Moses expounds the law, explains the basis for the covenant relationship between God and His people Israel, and applies it to the particular needs of the second generation (1:5). The Hebrew verb rendered "expound" is *be'er*, meaning "to make clear." Its use is rare, but its basic picture is "to dig" and is used to describe what is engraved, as letters on a stone (27:8; Hab. 2:2).[28] In Deuteronomy the law was expounded, but the Holy Spirit sought to deeply impress the revelation on the tables of the heart. Once the word of God was proclaimed, the people were reminded in a pointed way of their obligation to the revelation God had provided in the covenant.

## Outline

Introduction
  A. Title
  B. Deuteronomy: The Torah
  C. Structure
  D. Theology
  E. Date and Authorship
  F. Purpose and Theme
  G. Most Important Words
  H. Preamble of the Covenant: Moses' Opening Words

Chapter 1. The First Address: What God Had Done for Israel (1:6–4:43)
  A. Moses Recounts Israel's Experiences From Mount Horeb to Beth-Peor (1:6–3:29)
    1. From Horeb to Hormah: Defeat (1:6–46)
    2. The Journey Through the Trans-Jordan (2:1–25)
    3. The Conquest East of the Jordan River (2:26–3:11)

---

[27] J. B. Pritchard, ed., *The Ancient Near Eastern Texts*, (Princeton, NJ: Princeton University Press, 1955), pp. 238–239.

[28] William Gesenius, *Hebrew and Chaldee Lexicon*, ed. S. Tregelles, (Grand Rapids: Wm. B. Eerdmans Publishing Company, 1950), p. 100.

Chapter 4: The Third Address: An Appeal for the Covenant (29:1–30:20; Hebrew 28:68–30:20)
  A. An Appeal to Be Faithful (29:1–29; Hebrew 28:69–29:29)
    1. Reviewing the Past (29:1–8)
    2. A Call to Commitment (29:9–21)
    3. Teach, Teach, and Teach (29:22–29)
  B. Encouragement to Make the Right Decisions (30:1–20)
    1. The Promise of Restoration (30:1–10)
    2. Choose Life (30:11–16)
    3. Turn From Death (30:17–20)

Chapter 5. Moses' Last Words and His Death (31:1–34:12)
  A. The Law and Joshua (31:1–29)
    1. Encouragement by Moses and Presentation of Joshua (31:1–8)
    2. The Sabbatical Reading of the Law (31:9–13)
    3. The Charge to Moses and Joshua (31:14–29)
  B. Moses' Song (31:30–32:47)
    1. Introduction (32:1–4)
    2. A Complaint (32:5–6)
    3. The Mighty Acts of a Faithful God (32:7–14)
    4. The Indictment Against an Apostate People (32:15–18)
    5. The Judgment (32:19–25)
    6. God's Mournful Discourse (32:26–38)
    7. The Promise of Deliverance (32:39–42)
    8. A Call to Worship (32:43)
    9. Take Care How You Listen (32:44–47)
  C. Moses Sees the Land and Blesses the Tribes (32:48–33:29)
    1. Preparation for Death (32:48–52)
    2. Blessing the Tribes (33:1–29)
  D. Moses' Death (34:1–12)

**For Further Study**
    1. Using concordances, Bible Dictionaries, and commentaries, find the citations of Deuteronomy in the New Testament. Group these citations under doctrinal headings, e.g., the Word, God, Messiah, the Prophet and Prophecy, Israel, etc.

2. Do a word study of Deuteronomy's use of the words *Torah* (or *law*) *stipulations* (*'edut*), *decrees* (*hukkim*), and *laws* (*mishpatim*).

3. Study the basic thesis of Gerhard von Rad's form critical approach (in his commentary *Deuteronomy*). How would a conservative answer his position?

4. Why is similarity between the structure of Deuteronomy and the structure of the Middle Eastern suzerainty treaties important?

5. Trace the arguments between those who champion a second or first millennium B.C. dating for the Book of Deuteronomy.

6. Study the different possibilities for the dating of Deuteronomy and how the conservative position answers each of the arguments.

7. List the different possibilities for the authorship of Deuteronomy. What would a conservative's assessment be?

8. What are the basic doctrines in the major divisions of Deuteronomy?

9. Was John original in his statement, "This is love: not that we loved God, but that he loved us" (1 John 4:10)? Why or why not?

10. Some say that the Mosaic covenant sets up a tension between law and grace. Is this a fair assessment? How may the statement be corrected?

11. Why is the phrase "all Israel" important?

12. Study the geographical notations mentioned in the preamble (1:1–5).

# Chapter 1

---

## The First Address:
## What God Had Done for Israel
(Deuteronomy 1:6–4:43)

When God first called Moses to lead Israel from Egypt, he complained that he was "slow of speech and tongue" (Exod. 4:10). The reluctant shepherd had to be reminded that God Himself gave him his mouth and can make a person deaf and dumb as well as eloquent. Even then Moses complained in a desperate attempt to evade God's call. Whereupon the Lord angrily retorted that his brother Aaron would speak on his behalf. As the years passed, Aaron died (Num. 20:22–29), and Moses alone remained to address Israel. As we study Moses' speeches, we have an insight into his eloquence. God knew what He was doing when He called Moses to lead Israel out of Egypt, to instruct the nation in His ways, and to lead them to the very borders of the Promised Land. This story reminds us that when God calls us to a task, He knows us better than we realize. As we are faithful to His leadership, He will work through us to make a difference in the lives to whom we minister.

### A. Moses Recounts Israel's Experiences From Mount Horeb to Beth-Peor (1:6–3:29)

Middle Eastern treaties began with a historical prologue that indicated the events leading up to the treaty's ratification. In Deuteronomy, Moses likewise begins with a historical survey of Israel's experiences from the time they left Mount Horeb to the time they reached Jordan's east bank. Israel's knowledge of God came through two sources: revelation and specific historic acts. In the latter we see the faithful God who had worked in history to protect His people. The appeal, therefore, to the second generation was that they should give allegiance to their sponsor—God. Even though a first generation was unfaithful, God remained faithful to bring a second generation to the borders of Canaan.

### 1. From Horeb to Hormah: Defeat (1:6–46)

Moses' recollection includes brief discourses on past events, but the heart of the message reminds this second generation that their parents were unwilling to obey God.

**a. At Horeb (1:6–8).** Moses begins by first mentioning the covenant name for Israel's God, Yahweh (rendered LORD in our English translations).[1] To express the importance of this name, Moses reverses the usual order in Hebrew where the subject follows the verb. Here, the subject "Lord, our God" occurs first. Thus Moses underscores the significance of the covenant name.

Furthermore, this covenant name is personal: "LORD *our* God" or "LORD *your* God" occur a number of times in the book. In the linkage "your God . . . my people" we see from the outset a significant expression of grace in the covenant.

God had encouraged His people to move on from Horeb: "You have stayed long enough at this mountain. Break camp and advance" (1:6–7). Once the law had been given and the initial ratification of the covenant had been completed, the time came for the first generation to move on. At Horeb, one of the intentions of the covenant had worked to transform a slave people into a free people; the Israelites were now a nation. But a nation must find rest in its own land. God, therefore, had challenged His people to move out and occupy their own homeland. Possessing the land is an emphasis seen not only here but also at Mount Seir (2:3) and on the plains of Moab when Moses addresses the second generation.

As Moses had encouraged the people to move on from Horeb, he had described the Promised Land of Canaan and part of Syria (1:7). He told of 1) the hill country of the Amorites, which would be the central mountainous background of Judah and Ephraim; 2) the Arabah, which was the area north and south

---

[1] No pious Jew today will pronounce this name, but will use instead a substitute such as *Lord* or *Adonai.*

of the Dead Sea; 3) the western foothills, or the Shephelah, a range of low hills between the Judean mountains and the sea coast bordering the Mediterranean; and 4) the Negev, the dry land in the southern part of the land of Israel, from north of Beersheba to the Judean mountains, and running south to the head of the Gulf of Aqaba and west to Kadesh-Barnea. All of this area, extending along the sea coast as far north as Tyre and inland as far northeast as the upper regions of the River Euphrates, was land that the Lord had already promised to Abraham, Isaac, and Jacob (Gen. 15:18; 26:3; 35:12). Israel merely had to enter and take possession of it (1:8). The tie of land and seed is a theme that runs throughout the Book of Deuteronomy (1:35; 6:10, 18, 23; 7:13; 8:1; 9:5; 10:11; etc.).

**b. The Organization of Leaders and People (1:9–18).** Moses reminds the second generation that because Israel had increased to great numbers (from the days of the patriarchs until the experience at Mount Horeb and shortly thereafter), it was not possible for him to bear the burden of leadership alone (1:9). Moses refers to his father-in-law's advice to appoint assistants (Exod. 18:24). The wording in 1:9 is similar to Numbers 11:14, when Moses complained to God about his heavy responsibilities. God's advice had been to choose seventy elders who would also share the responsibility of leadership. However, no contradiction should be seen between the passages in Exodus and Numbers; the human and divine sources concurred about the need.

The reference to Israel becoming as numerous as the stars in the sky is intended as a hyperbole (1:10). Even so, the large population of Israel made it necessary for Moses to delegate the responsibility of leadership. The size of the Israelite nation fulfills God's promise to Abraham that his descendants would be as numerous as the stars of the heavens (Gen. 15:5). Although God had already kept His word, Moses wanted to see even greater numbers of people in future generations (1:11). His benediction, given in the name of "the LORD, the God of your fathers," suggests again God's special relationship with the fathers, the patriarchs. But He is also the God of the first generation that had come out from Egypt as well as the second generation that now stood on the plains of Moab. The emphasis is on the continuity of the people Israel and on God's word that He will fulfill His promise in each future generation.

Moses' recalls his frustration in being the sole leader of the nation (1:9) as he had sensed that with the increase of the population there would also be an increase in problems, burdens, and disputes (the Hebrew verb *riv* suggests cases of lawsuits). The people, therefore, had been asked to provide wise, understanding, and respected leaders from each of the tribes. The task would be difficult, but Israel needed leaders with the qualifications—wisdom, discernment, and knowledge—that would come only with years of experience (1:13).

The proposal had been readily acknowledged and accepted (1:14), and Moses had appointed leaders to exercise authority over Israel—commanders of thousands, hundreds, fifties, and tens (1:15). The nation was organized in military groupings, and its leaders exercised both judicial and military functions: "commanders" were experienced military men who could lead Israel's army into battle; "tribal officials" or "officers" were subordinate to the commanders and were used to administer justice and maintain civil order.

Moses recalls how he had also appointed judges (1:16) who exercised an impersonal judicial function in cases involving litigation between "brother Israelites" as well as between Israelites and aliens. Moses repeats the instructions for this sacred task: judges were to be impartial, hearing both small and great alike; they were charged to not be afraid of anyone because they represented the justice of God (1:17). Only when cases were too difficult for the judges would judicial action be passed on to Israel's leader. Such was the practice among the nations of the Middle East where kings adjudicated only the difficult cases. Since Israel was regarded as a theocracy, God was the King who acted through His official representative, Moses.

This section closes with a summary of what had happened at Horeb, referring only to what was necessary for the address to the second generation (1:18).

**c. From Horeb to Kadesh-Barnea (1:19–46).** Moses here narrates a summary of events described in Numbers 13 and 14. Israel had moved out from Horeb, passing through a vast and dreadful desert before they had reached Kadesh-Barnea (1:19). The journey of some one hundred miles in an area which was an almost waterless limestone plateau must have been difficult. The longer the people had journeyed, the more they had yearned for the Promised Land.

After the people had traversed this distance and had arrived at Kadesh-Barnea, they reached the hill country of the Amorites, the jumping off point into the Land of Promise. Moses recalls how he had charged Israel to enter in and take possession of the land (1:20–21). He had reminded Israel not to be afraid or discouraged. One cannot help but remember, however, the tragedy that occurred when that first generation failed to follow through on God's promises. Here Moses announces to the second generation that their parents had died in the wilderness over a period of thirty-eight years because of their rebellion and discontent.

Moses reminds the people how they had come to him, recommending that he send spies into the land (1:22). He hints at the Israelites' weak faith or even a lack of it. He had stressed the possibility of conquest, but the people had wanted to take practical measures and send spies into the land. At any rate Moses reminds them of how he had acceded, selecting one from each of the tribes (Num. 13:3–16). He had sent out the twelve to reconnoiter the land, advise on the best possibility for attack, and bring back information about the fertility of the land and the size of cities in it. Moses mentions the valley or wadi of Eschol, in the general area of Hebron. Evidently, there were many vineyards in the vicinity, and the fertility of the land and abundance of vineyards was in stark contrast to what the Israelites had just passed through in the terrible desert. Moses recalls that the spies had brought back a good report; indeed, the land was one flowing with milk and honey, and the evidence of a huge bunch of grapes was testimony to what God had in store for Israel (1:24–25).

But Moses reminds the second generation that their parents had rebelled against God (1:26). Instead of laying hold on God's promises, their parents had focused on the difficulties of conquering the land: 1) the Canaanites were stronger and taller; 2) the cities were large with walls to the sky; and 3) even the

Anakites were there (1:28)! Moses tells of how he had encouraged them, telling them not to be terrified or afraid; the Lord would go before and fight for them, even as He had done when He delivered them from Egypt. God's care in bringing that first generation to Kadesh-Barnea was like the love of a father carrying his child (1:29–31).

But they had completely perverted God's promises and love. Instead of believing God, the Israelites had grumbled in their tents, declaring that the Lord actually hated Israel and wanted to destroy the nation by delivering the people into the hands of the Amorites (1:27). In their rebellion they had developed a warped view of God's nature. They saw His love as hatred. They could no longer trust in the Lord their God in spite of His guidance with fire at night and a cloud during the day through the wilderness to Kadesh-Barnea (1:32–33). We, too, have our Kadesh-Barnea experiences as the Lord tests us to see if we will be faithful to Him. All of His resources are at our disposal, but commitment to His cause takes a wholehearted decision to trust Him in every circumstance.

The Lord had been angry with the first generation and had declared His judgment in an oath, proclaiming that only Caleb and Joshua would see the land of promise (1:34–36, 38). God had respected the faith of these two because they had encouraged Israel to attack immediately and take possession of the land (Num. 13:30). Some forty years later, Caleb was given land in the vicinity of Hebron, near the valley of Eschol, which he had earlier explored on foot (Josh. 15:13). The commendation came because "he followed the LORD wholeheartedly" (1:36).

Moses also remembers with shame the experience that had caused God to be angry with him (1:37) and that would prevent him from entering the Promised Land. Instead, Joshua the son of Nun would enter the land (1:38). Although Moses was not responsible for what happened to Israel at Kadesh-Barnea, his identification with Israel as their leader meant that he had to take responsibility for their failure. (Later, in 3:21–27, we see more specifically why Moses would not enter the land.) Even though Moses could not lead the second generation into Israel, he was responsible to commission Joshua and encourage and equip him to lead God's people in the conquest of their land.

Ironically, even though the first generation had been afraid that their offspring would be taken captive by the Canaanites, it was this second generation that would conquer the land (1:39). At that time, these offspring had been only children who could not distinguish between good and evil, an implication that the second generation had not been responsible for the failure of their parents.

Moses then recounted God's dreadful command to lead Israel through the desert "along the route to the Red [Reed] Sea" (1:40). This refers to the road which ran east of Kadesh-Barnea to Elath, a point on the Gulf of Aqaba. But the journey had turned out to be a roundabout march through the desert before Israel eventually came out to a point near to what today is the modern city of Eilat.

What was the first generation's reaction to God's oath? Moses sadly recounts how many Israelites seemingly had repented of their words and deeds at Kadesh-Barnea, declaring that they had sinned against the Lord (1:41). The tragedy was that they had lost an opportunity because of their rebellion and unbelief. Once God took the oath to keep them out of the Promised Land, it could only be presumption on their part to attack the Canaanites without His help. But many people had encouraged an attack anyway, thinking it would be easy to conquer the people of the land (1:41), even though Moses had told them not to go up and fight because the Lord would not support them (1:42). In their arrogance they had marched up to the hill country (1:43), but the Amorites had poured out of their cities and had chased the people like a swarm of bees, all the way to Hormah (1:44). The people who had remained then returned to Kadesh-Barnea to weep before the Lord, but God paid no attention and turned a deaf ear. What more was there to say? Victory could have been in their grasp if they had only been obedient to the plan of God. But after a humiliating defeat at the hands of the Canaanites, the first generation had to spend many days in the region of Kadesh (literally, "many days—all the time you spent there" 1:46).

## 2. The Journey Through the Trans-Jordan (2:1–25)

Moses' account describes how the second generation had come out of the Sinai wilderness area. Note the contrast between the obedience of the second generation and the rebellion of the first. The writer presents no dialogue. God issues His commands to conquer some areas and omit others, and Israel is obedient. Several phrases reflect a refreshing difference from the first generation: "get up" (2:13); "do not provoke" (2:5, 19); "we turned" (2:8b; 3:1); and "set out" (2:24).

**a. Mount Seir Experience (2:1–8).** After having been chased to Hormah, Israel had turned back on the road toward the Sea of Reeds to Kadesh-Barnea. They then had traveled southeast and had spent many days traveling along the hill country of Mount Seir, a region that was probably on the western borders of the Edomite territory (2:12). By this time, thirty-eight years had passed. It is difficult to trace Israel's exact movements, but finally God had instructed them to "turn north" (2:3). At that time Israel must have been somewhere near the southern end of Edom, and in turning north they could have traveled in two different ways: they could have passed around the eastern border of Edom, moving in the direction of Moab, or they could have proceeded along the western edge of Edom, going north through the Arabah and passing by the heights of Edom until they reached wadi Zered. They would have then turned east, going up the wadi until they finally could have turned north again to go around Moab (see 2:8).[2] We can only speculate about the route (2:4).

God had told Israel not to go through the territory of Edom. The account in Numbers 20:14ff. indicates how Edom refused to allow Israel passageway through their land, and Judges 11:17 recalls the same refusal by Edom, even while Israel had been still at Kadesh. The Lord had not wanted Israel to take any land from Edom (2:5). Moses' brief account described what actually occurred with Edom, that her land was not the Promised Land anyway. God had instructed the Israelites not to engage in battle with the Edomites, and whatever food and water were necessary

---

[2] Aharoni and Avi-Yonah, *Bible Atlas*, Map 53.

could be purchased from the Edomites, because water was extremely scarce on the route (2:6).

Moses reminds Israel that God had abundantly blessed His people with everything they had needed (2:7). Israel had no reason to take anything from Edom or even covet what they had. The writer describes the travel along the Arabah road, coming up from Elath and Ezion Geber, and traveling along the desert road of Moab. Once again, the location of the road is not certain. The road may be one that exists in the uninhabitable wilderness of Moab (1:8).

**b. Experiences with Moab and Ammon (2:9–25).** God also had told Israel to avoid the Moabites, who were descendants of Lot. Their land had already been assigned to them (2:9). 'Ar seems to be a synonym for Moab (see 2:18), although it could be one of the main cities of Moab (Num. 21:28).

The writer then provides a parenthetical statement about former inhabitants of the lands that Israel had passed through (2:10–12). The Emites, similar to the Anakites (see 1:28), were a tall people who lived in the territory that was conquered by Lot's descendants, the Moabites. The Emites were also the Rephaites. The Moabites preferred to call them Emites while the Ammonites called them Zamzummites (2:20–21). From earliest days, the Rephaites lived in the land of Israel (Gen. 15:20). It appears, however, that they were almost extinct by the time the Israelites had come into this particular territory (3:11). Later on, the Rephaites are described as shades or ghosts (2 Sam. 21:16, 18, 20, 22; 1 Chron. 20:6, 8), perhaps referring to the fact that they were long since gone.

The Horites used to live in the territory of Seir, but little is known of them (2:12). Even though the Hurrians were to have appeared in the second millennium B.C. in various parts of Syria and Israel, it is not clear whether the Hurrians are to be identified with the Horites.[3] We are told that the Edomites dispossessed the Horites, destroying them and possessing their land, even as Israel "did in the land the LORD gave them as their possession" (2:12). God, the Lord, has the prerogative to provide land for His people Israel as well as lands for other peoples.

---

[3] R. de Vauz, "Les Hurrites de l'histoire et les Horites de la Bible," *Revue Biblique*, (October, l967), pp. 481–503, as cited in Thompson, *Deuteronomy*, p. 92.

The story resumes as Moses recounts the route Israel had taken to cross the Zered Valley or wadi. It appears that Israel, by this time, had been at the southern border of Moab (2:13). Israel now had been obedient to the Lord, made significant by a historical note that thirty-eight years had passed since the days of Kadesh-Barnea when the first generation of fighting men had died out, even as the Lord had sworn (2:14).

Moses repeatedly mentions the fighting men of the first generation who had already died to emphasize the lesson that without faith, it is impossible to please God (2:16). The second generation had been faithful and had listened to His instructions, and as a result, they had been invincible on the march. After they had passed by the region of Moab at 'Ar (2:18), they had come to the territory of the Ammonites. Here God had once again warned them against harassing or fighting with these people. Rather, God had told them to pass on because He had given this land to another of Lot's descendants (2:19). Ammon occupied the area between the rivers of Arnon on the south and the Jabbok on the north, and so the Israelites had moved between them and Moab, along the Arnon, which was a common border for the two countries. Of necessity, Israel would have had to take some territory along the Arnon to get to the plains of Moab to where the second generation was now encamped.

The writer inserts another historical note, describing previous occupants of Ammon (2:20–23). They had been as numerous and as tall as the Anakites (2:21). *Zamzummites* is apparently not a Hebrew term, since Israel called these people Rephaites (2:11, 20). Another historical note refers to the Avvites who lived in southwestern Israel, even as far as Gaza, the city at the southwestern border of the land of Israel. These people had been driven out by the Caphtorites (possibly the Philistines), coming from Caphtor or perhaps Crete. The Dorian or Greek invasions of Crete (Josh. 13:3) had driven out the Philistines, or sea people, who then in the thirteenth century B.C. overran the Mediterranean seacoast.

The writer continues the historical narrative, sharing the Lord's directives for taking possession of the Promised Land (2:24–25). Israel had been instructed to pass through the Arnon Valley and capture this area. They became involved in a battle with Sihon, King of Heshbon, and his territory. This territory was an Amorite kingdom, covering an area north of the Arnon and extending from the Jordan River and Dead Sea on the west to the Ammonite territory on the east.

This second generation had a new experience with the Lord. The Lord had made the nations fear and tremble because of Israel's exploits. The reference to the nations who had heard reports of Israel would include not only this generation's victories but also God's exploits when He had delivered the first generation from Egypt, parting the Reed Sea. The news of these events had spread rapidly; Baalam had already referred to the Exodus and the events associated with it (Num. 23:22; 24:8). The crossing of the Arnon Valley marked the beginning of the capture of the promised homeland.

### 3. The Conquest East of the Jordan River (2:26–3:11)

**a. The Conquest of Heshbon (2:26–37).** To reach the plains of Moab, Moses had sent messengers from Kedemoth (on the edge of the desert) to Sihon, King of Heshbon, offering to pass peacefully on the highway as well as paying for food and water with silver (2:26–28). The payment could have been a lucrative one for Sihon, and the Israelite messengers had mentioned a similar experience with the Edomites and Moabites from whom Israel also bought food and water (2:29). However, Sihon had been of no mind to allow them to pass. God had made Sihon's spirit stubborn and his heart obstinate (2:30), even as He had done to Pharaoh years before. Both men, Sihon and Pharaoh, had been approached by God's servants, but these leaders had had no respect for peaceful consultations. When both leaders rejected peaceful offers, they had, in a sense, become God's adversaries.

Sihon's territory had run from the Arnon in the south, to the Jabbok River in the north. Its western borders had been the Jordan River and the Dead Sea. Part of this territory had already been taken by Sihon from the Moabites and remembered in a song of victory, the "Song of Heshbon" (Num. 21:27–30). Israel had been in the desert of Kedemoth, a wilderness area that was on the eastern border of Sihon's territory, and they probably had already entered in a few miles.

Moses recalls how when Sihon had refused (2:30), God had given the order for Israel to attack (2:31). The battle was known as the battle at Jahaz (2:32–34). There had been no question as to who would win this conflict because "the LORD our God gave him over to all of them" Moses says that the towns had been "completely destroyed," using a Hebrew term that referred to what is dedicated to the Lord for destruction. Everything had been completely given over to Him. Some people today raise questions about warfare that destroys not only towns but also men, women, and children. We must remember that Israel's God is the Holy One. The moral situation in the Middle East at the time was deplorable, and the Lord was outraged by the complete lack of morals among the people. His only resource was to bring judgment on nations and peoples for their reprehensible actions. Too often today we lose sight of God's holiness and righteousness. Only in contrasting to His holiness and the absolute wickedness of the people do we clearly see the only solution—the utter destruction of such evil people. On this occasion, however, Israel had been allowed to keep the livestock and plunder from the captured towns.

**b. Conquest of Bashan and Summation of Military Activity (3:1–11; see also Num. 21:33–35).** Bashan was possibly marked on its southern border by Gilead during the days of Og. Located east-northeast of the Sea of Galilee, it was a rich and fertile land whose prosperity was noted by Amos the prophet (Amos 4:1).

Israel had sent no messengers of peace to Og, who had marched out to meet them after he had heard of Sihon's defeat (3:1). God had encouraged Israel not to be afraid of Og, because he also would be handed over to them—his entire army and land (3:2). The short description of this battle tells us that Israel had struck down Og and his army, leaving no survivors (3:3). The victory had been a total success: Israel had captured sixty cities or walled settlements along with a number of unwalled settlements (3:5). The area of Argob (3:4) may have been an extremely fertile region within the larger kingdom of Og.

The writer concludes with a statement of the victory, reflecting God's faithfulness in handing over the land to them (3:6–7); cities and villages had been completely destroyed, and men, women, and children had been killed. And Israel had been permitted to keep the livestock and plunder for themselves.

Verse 8 emphasizes God's faithfulness in defeating both Bashan and Heshbon. The territory that Israel had conquered now extended from the Arnon Valley in the south (the southern border of the kingdom of Sihon) to Mount Hermon in the north. This mountain, which rose to over 9,000 feet, was called Sirion by the Sidonians (a fact also provided by the Ugarit texts) and Senir by the Amorites (supported in the Assyrian records of Shalmaneser).[4] The eastern limits of Bashan are indicated, "as far as Salecah," somewhere on the southern heights of Mount Hauran (3:10). The kingdom of Og had been an Amorite kingdom, while Og himself had been the last of the Rephaites (3:11). Og's huge bed (an iron couch approximately thirteen feet long, and six feet wide) had become his sarcophagus or burial bedstead. Verse 11 notes that the sarcophagus could still be seen in Rabbah in the territory of the Ammonites, possibly in the day when Deuteronomy was written. This information, however, could have been added later by an editor.

### 4. The Conquered Land Is Divided (3:12–22)

Moses had been permitted to see the conquest of the first part of the land, and he had supervised its distribution to the tribes who were to receive it.

Verses 12 and 13 provide a general statement about the territory allotted to Reuben and Gad. The land extended from Aroer on the bank of the Arnon Valley to half of the hill country of Gilead (3:12). The northern portion of this area was approximately what had once been the kingdom of Sihon. Furthermore, the half-tribe of Manasseh was given the rest of Gilead, all of what had once belonged to Og, the territory of Bashan (3:13).

The specifics of Manasseh's territorial subdivision follow in verses 14 and 15. Jair had received the northern part of Og's kingdom. It had consisted of Argob, whose northern and western limits had been the boundaries of the Geshurites and the Maacathites, a small city-state just south of Mount Hermon. This territory, named after Jair, had been called Havvoth Jair, meaning "settlements of Jair." To Makir, another sub-tribe of Manasseh, had been given the northern part of Gilead.

[4]Craigie, *Deuteronomy*, p. 120, n. 6.

Reuben and Gad had received the southern part of Gilead. It extended from the part of Gilead belonging to Makir to the south at the bottom of the Arnon Valley. On the east, a tributary of the Jabbok River marked the boundary with the Ammonites (3:16). The western border was the Jordan River, in the Arabah, from the Kinnereth or Sea of Galilee to the Sea of Arabah or the Dead Sea, "below the slopes of Pisgah." The "slopes of Pisgah" possibly refers to a certain point on a mountain range east of the sea—the point from which Moses was able to see territories west of the Jordan (3:27; 4:49; 34:1; Num. 21:20; 23:14).

Moses recalls that after he had divided the land east of the Jordan River, he had given orders to the two-and-a-half tribes, telling them that they were not to desert their brothers of the other tribes during the conquest of territories west of the Jordan River (3:18–20). The wives and children could remain in the cities and towns allocated to the two-and-a-half tribes, but the fighting men were commanded to cross over with the rest of the tribes "until the LORD gives rest to your brothers as he has given to you" (3:20). Moses had reminded the people that they were an inseparable unit.

Israel's leader had then challenged Joshua to ever remember God's faithfulness to Israel up to that point. The Lord had given victory to the second generation, and the land had been divided for two-and-a-half tribes on the east bank of the Jordan. Joshua, however, would be the man to lead Israel across the Jordan to conquer the rest of the Promised Land, and it was Moses' task to instruct his understudy about their future work (3:21–22). Moses reminded Joshua that he should not be afraid because God also would work mightily for Israel on the west bank.

### 5. Moses' Prayer to Cross the Jordan River (3:23–29)

Moses then bares his heart as he recalls how he once more had asked God if he could cross over and be in the land that had been promised to Israel (3:24–25). His moving prayer begins with a plea. The Hebrew words used here (the *hithpael* of *hanan*) emphasize a strong and solemn request for God to be compassionate with him (3:23). Moses had cried, "O LORD God," a phrase that appears only twice in Deuteronomy (3:24; 9:26

KJV). Abraham used this phrase as he prayed regarding the covenant (Gen. 15:2, 8) and Joshua used this same expression at one desperate point during the conquest (Josh. 7:7–9). In a sense Moses paid tribute to God as the One who had shown His servant His greatness and strong hand; no god in heaven or earth could do the great and mighty works by which God revealed Himself (3:24). Israel's leader had been bold in requesting permission from God to enter the Promised Land. The Lord takes great delight in such definite prayer.

But God had not granted the request. In fact, He had been angry with Moses because of the rebellion of the first generation (3:26). More specifically, however, God had been angry about Moses' behavior under pressure. Israel's leader had struck the rock for water when he had been told to speak to it (3:26; Num. 20:10–12). Moses had great faith that God could have given the land to the first generation as they were poised at Kadesh-Barnea, yet he was responsible for their acts. We might wonder why God would be very "angry" with His servant; the term is a strong one ("furious"), yet this kind of speech reflects a strong, intimate relationship between God and Moses whereby such deep feelings can be expressed. The Lord also had responded by saying, "Do not speak to me anymore about this matter," suggesting that Moses had persisted in his prayer, continually pounding the gates of heaven in order for God to relent.

Even though God would not allow Moses to enter the Promised Land, He had told him to go up to Mount Pisgah, located just east of the Dead Sea. There Moses would have a spectacular view of the land (3:27; see also 34:1). (Luke 9:28–31 tells us that Moses later appeared with Elijah on the Mount of Transfiguration. In a sense Moses was finally able to be in the land at the time when the Messiah Himself was present.)

Moses recounts how God had then told him to commission Joshua and encourage and strengthen him for the task of entry into the west bank (3:28). Moses displayed great tact and graciousness as he passed on the torch to Joshua.

The people had remained in the valley opposite Beth Peor. And while we are not certain about where it is located, the camp was probably east of the Jordan and opposite Jericho (3:29). Although Moses' death is not indicated until the end of the book, we can see how almost the entire account of Moses' teaching took place between the announcement of his death and its actual occurrence. Moses' great message and his own personal accounts are an eloquent testimony of how he was faithful to God in preparing Joshua and the second generation.

## B. Israel Must Obey God's Divine Instructions (4:1–40)

In Moses' first address, he recalls not only God's movement in history as He had delivered Israel from Egypt but also the experiences of the first and second generations until the latter was poised on the east bank of the Jordan River. Moses now provides a short message on the covenant and the law, which will introduce the Decalogue and other laws in his second message (5:1–28:68).

The structure of 4:1–40 closely parallels the structure of Middle Eastern treaties. Verses 1–2, 5, and 10 indicate the treaty's author. Thompson notes further parallels: mention of the preceding historical materials, the treaty's stipulations, the call for Israel to be obedient, the treaty's sanctions, the blessings and curses, the witnesses (26), and the necessity to share the treaty materials with the generations to come (10).[5] Although the literary form in chapter 4 does not exactly follow the legal form of the treaties, we can see many similarities in the way Israel's leader related God's message to His people.

### 1. Israel Must Listen and Obey (4:1–8)

Moses announces that he will teach the decrees and laws to this second generation (4:1). The request to follow the law did not ask for blind obedience to it, but rather the people needed to be willing to understand the Word and know what they were to do. These decrees and laws were the very life of the people as they sought to take the land which the God of their fathers was about to give them. Furthermore, the injunction that no one was to add to or subtract from God's instructions to Israel follows the formula of the treaties and law codes of other Middle Eastern literature in which no one was to tamper with the text of the agreements.[6] Deuteronomy was not to be regarded as final

---

[5] Thompson, *Deuteronomy,* p. 102.
[6] Craigie, *Deuteronomy,* p. 130. (See also 12:32 and Rev. 22:18–19).

revelation—the discourse about the institution of the prophet (18:15–22) established that further revelation was to be given through God's servants, the prophets. Regardless of which servants the word of God came through, it was to be viewed as sacred.

As a further reminder about commitment to God's divine instructions, Moses mentions the incident at Baal Peor (either at or near Beth Peor, 3:29) when a people had been disobedient to God's laws (Num. 25:1–9). The incident is a sordid one: Israelite men had committed adultery with the women of Moab, joining in the idolatrous worship of Baal (4:3–4). The penalty was harsh, but those who had remained faithful in the midst of temptation had been spared and were present at the time of Moses' address. The lesson was clear: Israel was to hold fast and remain ever close to the Lord.

Moses continues to encourage the people to be obedient to God's divine instruction (4:5–8). It would be the only way by which they could conquer the land, live in it, and be a testimony to other nations. Only as the Israelites would honor the Lord and commit themselves to His word would the nations know that God's people are wise and understanding. Through Israel's obedience, the pagan peoples would have opportunity to become believers. Moses recognized that Israel would one day be a great nation, but he further spells out why the nation would indeed be great: 1) the covenant relationship between the Lord and Israel; 2) God's closeness to His people, in contrast to the relationship between the false gods and the nations who believed in them; and 3) the righteous decrees and laws reflecting the holiness of God, in contrast to other unrighteous Middle Eastern law codes. God provided the best possible spiritual and moral relationships.

## 2. The Awesome Experience at Mount Horeb (4:9–14)

Moses again reminds the second generation of what had occurred at Mount Horeb. Many of the people had been mere children at the time they had stood with their parents in worship at the holy mountain, but now as mature people they were asked to remember carefully God's divine instructions or law. Not one word was to slip from their hearts as long as they lived (4:9).

How much more should we today obey the Word of God. We have a fuller revelation of Israel's Messiah, Jesus, who died for our sins. Because of His resurrection, we can experience the power to live godly lives. The responsibility, therefore, rests even more heavily on us.

Moses also calls on that second generation to recall the awesome sight at Mount Horeb. The mountaintop had blazed with fire and had been enveloped by black clouds and deep darkness (4:11); the Lord had spoken from the midst of the fire, but no form had been visible (4:12). That sight had been terrifying to the first generation, and it would have been an even more moving experience to the children. Moses reminds the people that God had directed him to teach them the decrees and laws they were to follow in the Promised Land (4:13–14). Merely reading about the experience had a profound effect on many of the people in subsequent history as they sought to express something of God's awesome presence (Deut. 33:2; Judg. 5:5: Ps. 68:8; and Hab. 3:3).

### 3. A Dire Warning Against Idolatry (4:15–31)

Moses admonishes the people, warning them not to make any idol that would represent God. The people were not to corrupt themselves by fashioning idols or images of any shape, male or female (4:16). To do so would be disobedient to the second commandment. The injunction was serious; while God is certainly personal, the danger would be to represent Him in some human likeness which would only be a perversion. To bring Israel's God down to the human level would only limit Him. He is not a being who can be limited in any way.

Other warnings follow: God is not to be conceived in the likeness of any animal, bird, creeping thing that moves on the ground, or fish in the water (4:17–18). The Israelites were familiar with the Egyptian pantheon, wherein the likenesses of gods and goddesses were conceived in the form of cats, birds, dogs, crocodiles, bulls, etc. They had already been caught in one such situation (Exod. 32) when they worshiped a god made *in the form* of the Egyptian bull.

Moses also warns Israel not to make any forms or images of gods representing the heavenly bodies—the sun, moon, and stars (4:19). The worship of heavenly bodies was prevalent among the Hittites, Egyptians, Assyrians, and other nations of the Middle East. The danger was to take the created bodies of the physical world and turn them into objects of worship.

Moses reminds the people that God had delivered them from Egypt, the iron-smelting furnace, to become a distinct nation, different from all other nations (4:20). The Egyptian experience had been nothing but pain and suffering, but the Lord in His power and graciousness had released His people from that period of horror. But for what purpose? The nation was to regard itself as the people of His inheritance, a phrase occurring in a number of other passages (7:6; 14:2; 26:18). They were not to become proud and self-righteous as a result, but they were to realize that they had been called by His grace. Therefore, the consequences of any misbehavior were serious, because it meant flouting God's special care for them.

Moses once more painfully recounts that he would not enter the Promised Land because of the disobedience of that first generation (4:21–22). He ruefully declares that he will have to die on the east bank. But Moses points out that he wants Israel to remain pure and lay hold of all the blessings God wishes to give them. In view of their special position, they were not to forget the covenant of the Lord their God and turn away from their special relationship with Him to make idols which He had forbidden (4:23). If they should apostatize, they would learn that He is a jealous God and a consuming fire (4:24). Such language is indeed stern, but He is zealous for His righteousness, and Israel must not spurn His love. To make images and idols would only mean that they found His love inadequate.

Israel's lawgiver grew apprehensive as he thought of what could happen to the nation once they achieved all that God had to offer in a land of plenty. He had lived long enough and was astute enough in his judgment of human nature to know that in the midst of plenty, the hearts of the people could be turned away. The danger was that they could very well forget their God and seek the pagan gods and goddesses of the nations (4:25). Faced with such a prospect, Moses called heaven and earth as witnesses against his audience and their descendants for any action that would provoke the Lord (4:26). Such was the procedure in the Middle Eastern treaties, where witnesses were to be summoned in case of any wrongdoing. Moses warns the people that disobedience would result in national death (4:26), exile from the land, and scattering among the nations (4:26–27). (This is further spelled out in chapter 28.)

Moses elaborates about what will happen if God's people should be unfaithful in their worship. Exile was to take place. But for what purpose? Many people point to the exile of northern Israel after the fall of Samaria (2 Kings 17:6) and the exile of Judah after the fall of Jerusalem (2 Kings 24:14ff.; 25:10ff.) to emphasize that this was God's judgment on His people. But more is involved. The point is that if Israel would be exiled in a foreign land and would see the emptiness of pagan worship, then a remnant would turn to the true and living God and seek Him with all their heart and soul. In such distress, God promised to restore His people and bring them back to their land. He is a merciful and gracious God and will ever remember the covenant He has with them. Never will He abandon the nation for as long as there is a history of mankind (4:27–31 and Gen. 17:7).

### 4. Israel, God's Chosen People (4:32–40)

Moses had called heaven and earth to witness God's righteous action in judging His disobedient people. Now, however, the heavens are witness to God's unique action in calling a people who were the smallest nation on earth (7:7), bringing them out of Egypt, and revealing Himself to them in a special way at Sinai as He spoke there from out of the fire (4:32–33). Israel's leader raises a pointed rhetorical question: Was there ever a time when a people heard God's voice speaking out of the fire as Israel had heard (4:33)? Which God had ever taken for Himself a nation out of another nation (Egypt) and by signs, wonders, war, a mighty outstretched arm, and great awesome deeds revealed Himself in such a way (4:34)? The only response had to be negative—no god had ever worked wonders and miracles as the Lord did for Israel.

Could any in Israel, particularly that second generation, ever say that God did not exist? Could the first generation dare to say that God did not exist? The tragedy was that although the first generation would never say God was non-existent; they chose to disobey Him (4:35).

For Israel, the two basic sources of knowledge of God's existence were: 1) the Exodus and 2) the revelation of God at Mount Sinai. Since Mount Sinai, God has given us one more source in the person and work of Jesus Christ (2 Cor. 4:4).

Moses declares that God had loved their forebears and had chosen them, bringing them out of Egypt. But His work had not stopped with the deliverance of the first generation. The second generation had also experienced His love and seen His power as He began to drive out nations greater and stronger than they, making possible the beginning of the promise to inherit the land (4:37–38). God is real; He is the God of heaven and earth, and no other god can display such power or give such love.

Because Israel was God's chosen people, they were to acknowledge Him as the Lord. He is the God in heaven above and on the earth below (4:39). Moses challenges the people to yield their allegiance to the sovereignty of God and to keep His decrees and commands which He provided so that it would go well with them. If Israel would be obedient to the law, not legalistically, but with love, they would live long on the land and enjoy all His bounty and blessing.

## C. The Cities of Refuge (4:41–43)

Notice that these instructions about the cities of refuge are not a part of Moses' actual address. They are presented in the third person and can be seen as an appendix or something provided before the second address in which the law is expounded.

The instructions, very similar to those given in Numbers 35:6–32, describe three cities set apart on the east bank, one in each of the three parts—the southern, central, and northern areas. Moses gives the location of the three cities: Bezer, in the territory of Reuben, is difficult to locate; Ramoth in Gilead is in the center part, between the rivers Yarmok and Jabbok; Golan, on the modern Golan Heights, is in the territory of Manasseh, in Bashan, but once again the specific site is not clear.

These cities of refuge provided an asylum for anyone who innocently caused another person to die. Before the law was given, it was easy for clans to take revenge on the offenders who killed one of their own; but now with the establishment of the law, proper legal procedures were instituted to protect the life of an innocent person.

## For Further Study

1. Study the route the Israelites took in their movement from Kadesh-Barnea to the plains of Moab on the east bank.

2. Study the battles Israel fought with the Midianites, Sihon of Heshbon, and Og of Bashan. Study the nations and the territories involved.

3. Analyze some of the reasons why the first generation failed at Kadesh-Barnea.

4. Study both occasions when water came out of the rock (Exod. 17:1–7, Num. 20:1–12). List the reasons why Moses was not permitted to enter the Land of Promise.

5. Study the origins of Edom, Moab, and Ammon as well as the boundaries and territories those people occupied.

6. Ascertain the origin of the Rephaites. Why in later history does this word come to mean "shades" or "ghosts"?

7. Draw a map showing the division and subdivision of the land on the east bank and the two-and-a-half tribes of Israel.

8. Why is the warning against idolatry so serious?

# Chapter 2

---

# The Second Address:
# The Law of God—Part One
(Deuteronomy 4:44–11:32)

Moses' second message, a lengthy one, is the very heart of the book. We note once more the parallels to the Middle Eastern treaties which began with the historical prologue and the stipulations (both general and specific) of the agreement between the king and the subjects. Moses followed this cultural pattern, providing Israel with the call for total allegiance to the Lord, first in general statements (chap. 5–11) and then with more precise terms in the second part of the message (chap. 12–28). For the sake of convenience, we will examine the second message in two parts.

## A. Introduction (4:44–49)

These verses serve as an introduction, summarizing the historical events described in the preceding chapters. Perhaps Moses had taken a break after his first address and felt the need to provide a brief summary before he launched into the tremendous possibilities the covenant faith can provide for a godly lifestyle.

Once again we note terms which are extremely important in the covenant (4:44–45): "law" (Torah), "stipulations, decrees and laws" (see previous discussion). Moses is not proposing a new covenant; rather he expounds upon and explains further the covenant provided at Mount Horeb.

Moses summarizes Israel's recent history: 1) how and why they finally arrived at Beth Peor, 2) the tremendous victories over Sihon and Og, and 3) taking possession of their territory for

Reuben, Gad, and the half-tribe of Manasseh. The boundaries of the two-and-a-half tribes are mentioned, extending from the edge of the Arnon Valley north to Mount Hermon, called in Hebrew, "Siyon," which is the same as "Sirion" (3:9; Ps. 29:6).

## B. The New Life Within Covenant Faith (5:1–11:32)

In addition to the historical prologue, Middle Eastern treaties include a section of stipulations, first basic and then detailed. Following this form, Moses outlines the Lord's guidelines—first in basic principles (chap. 5–11), then in detail (chap. 12–28).

### 1. The Covenant Faith and its Unique Moral Standard (5:1–6:3)

The very heart of covenant faith is the Decalogue. It is not merely a call for a legalistic response, but rather it defines the possibility for a close-knit relationship between the nation and her God.

**a. The Call to Listen (5:1–5).** Immediately in the first verse, Moses uses verbs which serve as the introduction to the Decalogue: *hear, learn, be sure,* and *follow* (5:1). Moses carefully prepares his audience for the moral standard that represents a divine righteousness that in turn reflects the God who is holy. Another striking phrase, "Hear, O Israel," is used several times to announce important items (6:4; 9:1; 20:3; 27:9). Moses calls the people to pay attention to the decrees and the laws already presented to the first generation at Mount Horeb. Nevertheless, the second generation is connected to the first generation by "the LORD our God" who made the covenant, ensuring that each generation has a living relationship with God through the covenant (5:2–3).

Moses recalls once more for Israel their experience at Mount Sinai, when God had spoken to them "face to face out of the fire on the mountain" (5:4). There is no contradiction to 4:12 where the people heard the voice of God speaking directly to them but did not see any form. Moses reminds his audience again that he was indeed the mediator between the Lord and Israel, declaring His word to the nation (5:5). His was the unique privilege to speak to God who appeared to him in some form of theophany. Moses could even have spoken to a pre-incarnation form of the Messiah.

**b. The Decalogue (5:6–21).** These verses contain ten covenant "words," or Ten Commandments (Exod. 20:1–17), and in time, the Decalogue takes on ever-increasing importance as the prophets, Writings, and rabbis continually refer to it. On many occasions, Jesus Himself refers to the Decalogue (Matt. 5:21, 27, 33; Mark 12:29–31; Luke 10:27; 18:20). The writers of the New Testament also had numerous opportunities to refer to the commandments (Rom. 2:21–22; Gal. 5:19ff.; Eph. 4:28; 5:3; Heb. 4:9; James 2:11; etc.). Church leaders throughout the centuries have highly regarded the Decalogue because it reflects a moral standard that is absolute.

The Decalogue may be viewed in two parts: one's reponsibility to God and one's responsibility to other people. A right relationship to God must come first, and only then can a person serve other people in a way pleasing to God. The first four commandments emphasize that God is sovereign, calling on each person to respond to His identity, nature, and name as well as the day to worship Him. The last six commandments deal with each person's obligation to parents (and therefore to God), to view life as sacred, to respect people and property, and to care for one's relationship with other people.

God never demanded that people follow these commandments in a legalistic sense; to do so only warps the concept God had in mind for a new life within a covenant relationship. His primary design was that people should first be born again and then the Decalogue can serve as a guide by which to live a holy life and serve others.

The Decalogue also provides a moral standard for individuals as well as nations. God will one day judge both individuals as well as nations by this particular standard. No individual or national leader will ever say that he or she did not have access to God's moral standard; the moral standard is ever present, and God holds people and nations responsible to it.

The Decalogue was and is, in an emphatic sense, the means to remind people when they fall short of God's righteousness. When people commit crimes against other people as well as sin against God, the Holy Spirit is ever present to convict people of

their need for forgiveness. For Israel, God in His mercy
provided the sacrificial system within the covenant so that
people could find the Lord through the sin offering (Lev.
4:1–5:13). Today the Holy Spirit points to the sacrificial death of
Jesus, who made atonement for sin and appeals to offenders to
find forgiveness in Him.

One more word about the Decalogue. Many Christians
assert that we now live in the age of grace and that the Old
Testament dispensation was the age of law. In response to that
claim, we must remember several guidelines: First, people were
never born anew apart from grace, whether in Old or New
Testament times; no one has ever been saved by law. Second,
we must recognize the different uses of the word "law." "Law"
refers to the Old Testament itself: 1) the first five books of
Moses; 2) the prophets (1 Cor. 14:21); and 3) the psalmic
writings (John 10:34). Because Paul and Jesus referred to the
respective portions of the Old Testament as "the law," the
entire Old Testament is the "written law." Furthermore, the
moral element (or Decalogue) of the Mosaic covenant is
repeated in the New Testament. The only omission in Paul's
letters is the day of the Sabbath worship, apparently leaving the
day of worship open to satisfy Christians' particular cultural or
practical needs. In the West, believers worship on the first day
of the week because of a traditional preference set in motion as
early as 500 A.D., but modern Jewish believers in Israel have
their day of rest and worship on the seventh day, or Sabbath.
Many believers in Muslim countries have set aside Friday as
their special day. When a person is born again, whether in Old
or New Testament times, the moral standard is written on the
heart. The Decalogue, then, is important because it enables a
person to understand the lifestyle that pleases God.

The phrase "I am the LORD your God" (5:6) marks the One
who originated the covenant, quite similar to the opening
statement in any Middle Eastern treaty. The rest of this passage
describes the historical events associated with the treaty; the
Lord, the real God, is the One who brought Israel out of Egypt
and identified Himself to this second generation, attesting to the
moral lifestyle Israel is called on to live. The Lord is the
authority behind the Decalogue.

**(1) The First Commandment (5:7).** In the opening statement, the Lord had reminded Israel that He is the only God; the gods of other nations are to be of no interest to Israel. He was the God who had delivered her from Egypt and had made possible the victories on the east bank of the Jordan River. It was to this holy and protecting God that Israel was to yield her allegiance. Israel's worship system was to be monotheistic; the Lord does not permit any rivals.

Because God put the commandment in such a way, it should also have its impact on every sphere of life: what kind of food was to be eaten (14:3–21); the warning against idolatry (chap. 13); and the call to destroy all pagan sanctuaries and pagan gods (7:5; 12:3). The phrase "before me" has been translated in a number of ways: "besides me," "at my side," and "against me." But no matter how some critics want to suggest that Israel's God was first among many gods, the implication of the covenant is that Israel is to have nothing to do with the pagan gods. The nation is to worship only the true God.

**(2) The Second Commandment (5:8–10).** This passage is similar to Exodus 20:4–6. Israel was prohibited from having any false idea about the worship of the Lord. Israel was warned not to be like other nations who worshiped animals, birds, creeping things, and the heavenly bodies (4:15–19). Idol worship will only pervert the concept of the real God.

The second commandment further reminds Israel not to bow down to any images or idols of pagan gods and worship them. The phrase "bow down" conveys the picture of complete submission. We live in a day when many of God's people have lost the concept of what worship means; they no longer live in total submission to God alone.

Israel was reminded that the Lord is a jealous God, zealous for His holiness and righteousness. He requires total allegiance and does not tolerate rivalry with any false god or goddess. God's people were not to pervert their allegiance to the Lord, and if they did, He had a way of exacting His judgment, even to the third and fourth generation of those who would turn their backs on Him. The covenant relationship was intended to reflect a loving relationship between God and His people, enabling countless generations to love Him.

The same kind of phraseology is found in the Middle Eastern treaties. Kings expected allegiance from their subjects, who then could expect great blessings. But when subjects became disobedient, they lost the possibility of blessing and could also expect severe judgment from their king.

(3) **The Third Commandment (5:11).** Israel was instructed to refrain from a careless use of the *name* of the Lord. God revealed Himself to Israel through His name, the Lord (*Yahweh*), as an indication of His intimacy with His people. Therefore the misuse of God's name was very serious. People had the high privilege of making promises and calling on His name to help them in their godly desires, but unfortunately, His name was also used for purely selfish motives. This was forbidden.

In the ancient pagan world, some kind of magical power was assumed to be attached to the name of a deity, as was illustrated when Balak called on Balaam to curse Israel in the name of Israel's God (Num. 22–24). But such practices were forbidden because "the LORD will not hold anyone guiltless who misuses his name" (5:11).

(4) **The Fourth Commandment (5:12–15).** Although this commandment about the Sabbath is expressed positively (in contrast to the first three which are negative), it does have negative implications.

Note some differences in terminology between this expression of the fourth commandment and the one found in Exodus 20:8–11. Deuteronomy 5:12 uses the word "observe" from the Hebrew *shamor*, meaning "take care"; Exodus 20:8 uses the word "remember." Deuteronomy 5:12b adds the phrase "as the LORD your God has commanded you" to what is stated in Exodus 20:8. Deuteronomy 5:14 adds "your ox, your donkey" and "any" to what is recorded in Exodus 12:10. These additions do not change God's intentions; Moses was interpreting the commandment for the situation once Israel had settled on the land.

The fourth commandment gives two reasons for observing the Sabbath: 1) Exodus 20:11 states that because God rested on the seventh day after creating the world (Gen. 2:2), the people were also to follow His example and set aside the seventh day for rest. In addition, the commandment recognizes that people need to rest in order to be renewed, and God through His providence makes that kind of rest possible; 2) Deuteronomy states that Israel should observe the Sabbath because God had delivered them from servitude in Egypt, and they were now a free people. They could, therefore, rest from all of their labors while remembering their deliverance from Egypt. As a further note, not only were the Israelites told to rest on the Sabbath, but their animals, their servants, and the aliens or non-Israelites within their city gates also were instructed to rest from their work.

It has always been difficult for Israelites to keep this commandment (see Neh. 13:15–22). Therefore, by the time of Jesus, the religious leaders had added many laws to the Sabbath system, which were no doubt intended to encourage the people to remember the Sabbath. But the day of rest became the occasion for observing a minutia of laws, and Jesus was forced to declare that the Sabbath was made for man, and not man for the Sabbath (Mark 2:27–28). Lest we become self-righteous, we must also remember that many people within the church today have a multiplicity of unwritten laws on how Sunday should be observed and what should or should not be done.

By the fourth century, the church set aside the first day of the week to commemorate the resurrection of Jesus, and in the statements in the general councils, the observance of Saturday was prohibited.[1] Yet, since no reference was ever made as to which rest should be observed in the New Testament, this writer feels God gives believers an honest freedom of choice. Aside from which day is observed, the principle is that both individuals as well as national leaders must allow one day in seven for the human body to rest and change the everyday pace and activities. For believers, particularly, this is the day to worship the Lord.

**(5) The Fifth Commandment (5:16).** The fifth commandment is known as a commandment with a blessing: "that you may live long." Although the commandment in Deuteronomy is almost identical to the one in Exodus, Moses adds here, "that it may go well with you in the land. . . ."

---

[1] Philip Schaff, *History of the Christian Church*, III, (Grand Rapids: Wm. B. Eerdmans Publishing Company, 1950), pp. 378–86.

The fifth commandment implies that the family is the basic unit of society, and children are to preserve that unit by honoring their parents. Even as small children learn to respect and honor their father and mother, they can also be taught to focus on God, know Him as a heavenly Father, and honor Him. So as to emphasize the responsibility, the commandment also promises the blessings of long life to those who will observe it.

**(6) The Sixth Commandment (5:17).** The remaining five commandments are designed to teach the people how God wants them to relate to others within society. First of all, one is to have a fundamental respect for the sanctity of life, and murder is prohibited. The Hebrew word used here is *rasah*, which means "to kill a person," which includes premeditated murder, manslaughter, or accidental killing. Deuteronomy 19:1–13 provides guidelines for settling issues involved in manslaughter and accidental killing.

The sixth commandment is based on the idea expressed in Genesis 9:6, that "whoever sheds the blood of man" has decreased the image of God in that person. When someone kills another person, God's image is actually marred. In this sense, God has put a special premium on the value of a human life.

The sixth commandment does not prohibit capital punishment, as we shall see in Deuteronomy 17:2–7 and 19:12. We sometimes become so taken up with the "horror" of taking a person's life in capital punishment that we have overlooked the fact that the offender has already taken the life of another person. Neither does the commandment prohibit war, as we shall see in Deuteronomy 20.

**(7) The Seventh Commandment (5:18).** The commandments call not only for respecting the sanctity of life, but also the sanctity of marriage. To preserve the marriage, the commandment called for impeccable behavior of husbands and wives in their relationships with the opposite sex (Deut. 22 and 24 discuss the guidelines for illicit sexual behavior). The seventh commandment seeks to curb unacceptable sexual relationships. This legislation was not unique to Israel. Immorality was also regarded as a social evil in other Middle Eastern societies.[2]

---

[2]Thompson, *Deuteronomy*, p. 118.

The seventh commandment was also a warning to Israelites who, after settling down in the land, would find themselves enticed by the pagan's false worship that included the satisfaction of sensual desires. More than any other reason, the involvement with pagan nations and their deplorable practices was the downfall of the nation in the first commonwealth. The primary purpose of the commandment was to provide for a faithfulness between a husband and wife in the marriage relationship, in which both partners were completely committed to the God of Israel.

(8) **The Eighth Commandment (5:19).** Middle Eastern countries considered theft a social sin. At first one might feel that this is merely a prohibition against unlawfully acquiring property, already mentioned in Exodus 22:1–13. But the commandment's primary purpose was for people to have so much respect for one another that a neighbor's property would be regarded as sacred.

Another dimension of stealing was the kidnapping of people (Deut. 24:7), an even more serious matter because human life was involved.[3] Kidnapping for personal gain was prevalent in the Middle East because slaves were acquired this way. But to separate an Israelite from his or her family was also a crime because the Israelite was not only sold to another nation but was also severed from the covenant relationship. Obviously, if the kidnapped person was a believer, his or her faith remained intact even though he or she was cut off from the rest of Israel. Kidnapping today is still a violation of this commandment, because one is stealing from a person what rightfully belongs to him or her.

(9) **The Ninth Commandment (5:20).** False testimony, or witnessing against one's neighbor, is also prohibited. When one gives such testimony, a person's future is jeopardized. In the worst possible situation, a false word could even commit a person to the sentence of death. Lying under oath in court is quite prevalent even in today's system of justice.

But not only is one to give correct testimony in a court of law. He or she is to act with integrity toward his or her neighbor

---

[3] Craigie, *Deuteronomy*, p. 161.

in every aspect of daily life within the community of God. Such a standard must also prevail among Christians today.

(10) **The Tenth Commandment (5:21).** The arrangement of this command differs from Exodus 20:17. In the latter passage, the neighbor's house is mentioned first, followed by the injunction not to covet the neighbor's wife. In the Deuteronomy passage, coveting the neighbor's wife is mentioned before coveting the neighbor's house or land. Moses was perhaps quite sensitive about a man's attitude toward women. A man must regard as sacred the tie of a neighbor's wife and her husband. This is a factor also mentioned in other passages (Deut. 21:10–14; 22:13–19; 24:1–5).

The tenth commandment, unlike the other nine, deals with a person's motivation. Motives are difficult to judge because they lie buried deep in the heart. One cannot see crimes and sins of the heart. Only when a person actually has committed a crime or sin can the offender be convicted. Nevertheless, God's directive is for everyone to deal with inner motives. When inner thoughts and desires are right, then the regard for a fellow human being will also be proper. Jesus addressed Himself to this evil of coveting (Matt. 5:21–48) as He reinforced it; not only was an evil deed to be judged, but one must also judge the wrong desires that can lead to the deplorable deeds.

c. **Moses Explains His Role at Mount Horeb (5:22–33).** After Moses presents the Decalogue to the second generation, along with his additional comments, he once more recounts his experiences at Mount Horeb when the commandments and other features of the law were given.

(1) **Moses Is Asked to Be the Mediator (5:22–27).** Moses concludes his discussion about the Decalogue by saying that the Lord had proclaimed these commandments (these words) in a loud voice on Mount Horeb, "out of the fire, the cloud and the deep darkness," which suggests an awe-inspiring encounter (5:22). God Himself had given the Decalogue (4:2), and He affixed these words on stone tablets and delivered them to Moses. (The Decalogue will be considered in a more detailed form in 9:9–10:5.) Moses also stated that God had added nothing more to the commandments, suggesting that the Decalogue is a complete statement of the covenant. The rest will be

commentary, interpretation, and further explanation of what the Decalogue means.

Because of the holy presence of the Lord, when "the mountain was ablaze with fire," the elders and the heads of the tribes had been moved by deep fear and had asked Moses to represent the nation before God and also be its mediator (5:24–27). They had been impressed by the glory and majesty of the "living God" who had spoken out of the fire. Now, some thirty-eight years later, Moses was also the mediator to the second generation; they also recognized the honor that had been conferred on him by their fathers.

(2) **God's Comment and Instructions to Moses (5:28–31).** God had heard the first generation's request that Moses be their representative, and He had approved it, exclaiming, "Oh, that their hearts would be inclined to fear me . . . always" (literally, "O that their heart . . . fear me . . . all the days"). Only in following His word would the best welfare of the nation be preserved. God then had told Moses that the leaders of Israel should return to their tents, but that His servant should remain on the mountain to receive His commands, decrees, and laws which were then to be shared with the people.

(3) **Again the Charge to Israel (5:32–33).** Having received the word in such awesome circumstances, the people of Israel were to follow carefully what had been commanded them through their mediator, Moses. But the real authority for the revelation had been God Himself. Therefore, the people had a responsibility to listen and obey so that they could prosper and enjoy all that God had prepared for them in His land. The second generation was now the recipient of the benefits mentioned so many years before at Mount Horeb.

**d. Introduction to the Great Commandment (6:1–3).** These three verses serve as an introduction to the heart of the covenant's explanation of Israel's relationship with God. Moses begins by stating that "these are the commands, decrees, and laws." Actually the word "commands" is singular (*miṣwah*) in Hebrew. In a sense, the *miṣwah* is a charge, to be explained further by the statutes and commandments and expanded later in chapters 12–26. The directives given to the first generation at Mount Horeb (5:22–23) are repeated on the east bank of the

Jordan to a second generation (6:1–3). The people were to be obedient, in order that it may go well with them and that they "may increase greatly in a land flowing with milk and honey." The last phrase is mentioned a number of times—four times in Exodus, once in Leviticus, four times in Numbers, five times in Deuteronomy—and also is known in other Middle Eastern literature that describes this very land.[4]

### 2. Love for God and its Meaning for Every Family (6:4–9)

**a. Love the Lord (6:4–6).** In the very heart of Israel's confession, the nation was to completely repudiate the gods and goddesses of the pagans and acknowledge that their God is indeed one. God's people were to love Him with all their being; they were to remember, however, that if they would ever share their allegiance or love for the Lord with other gods and goddesses, then their misguided actions would be considered an affront to the one holy and true God.

Israel was called on to "hear" (in the imperative mood, 6:4). The phrase, "Hear, O Israel" (5:1, 6:3) is a challenge to consider the great truth that the Lord is one. The passage is known to Jewish people as the *Shema* (Hebrew word meaning "hear") and is recited along with 11:13–21 and Numbers 15:37–41 in the daily morning prayer. Ever since the Babylonian exile, Jewish people have affirmed the one great truth that their God is indeed one.

There is no contradiction between this confession and the New Testament doctrine of the triunity of God; however, a full-blown revelation of the New Testament should not be read back into the Old. During Old Testament times, Israel was in the midst of a sea of paganism and was being schooled in the truth of the oneness of God. In a later and more full revelation (the Incarnation), God's people were given a deeper appreciation for His oneness and His composite unity. And yet, the Hebrew word *'ehad,* which is rendered "one" in English, lends itself to the interpretation of God as a composite unity (see also Gen. 2:24, where the word "one," *'ehad,* does intimate a plurality of persons).

---

[4]J. B. Pritchard, ed., *Ancient Near Eastern Texts*, pp. 18–25, lines 80–90, where the Egyptians describe the northern part of Israel by this very phrase.

The Israelites were asked to love the Lord their God (6:5). And their allegiance to Him was not to be based on mere legalism, in do's and don'ts, but rather on a deep relationship based on love. Even in the Middle Eastern treaties between subjects and king the phrase of "love for the king" was an important one, but the biblical concept of love has a deeper meaning.

The extent of this love was to affect every level of a person's being. They were told to love God "with all your heart and with all your soul and with all your strength" (Deut. 4:29; 6:5; 10:12; 11:13; 13:3; 26:16; 30:2, 6, 10). The words "heart," "soul," and "strength" reflect an insight into biblical psychology. "Heart" refers to one's mind and will and is also to be regarded as the seat of the emotions; "soul" includes a person's very life and being; and "strength" refers to how a person can love the Lord with all his or her might.

The appeal was for Israel to have the commandments on their hearts (6:6). If they would love the Lord, then out of their hearts would come the choices to live the commandments or word which God had revealed to them. Morals can never be legislated, but a heart of love for the Lord will produce the choice to live morally in accordance with His wishes. Obviously, only the remnant in Israel who were born again could really appreciate and live what 6:5–6 envisions.

**b. Each Family's Love for God (6:7–9).** Parents were to teach their children about God's commandments and were to help them love the Lord. Parents were to talk about God's Word and its requirements throughout the day—in the home, along the road, and from early in the morning until they went to bed at night (6:7). Parents were to teach their children the meaning of the commands, decrees, laws, statutes, and ordinances, so that the children could understand them. Each one who is born again is equipped to live this word. Deuteronomy suggests that spiritual training does not begin when a person is in the teen years but when a person is a young child. And the setting of that early spiritual training is in the home; parents are the most important spiritual teachers (4:9b; 6:20–25; 11:19).

Moses instructs the people to tie the commandments as symbols on their hands and foreheads and to write it on the door frames of their houses and gates (6:8–9). In later practice, Jewish people took these passages in a literal sense. Jewish men wore phylacteries (*tefilin*), which were little cubes attached to a wider, rectangular base that allowed for the insertion of a small parchment on which was written Deuteronomy 6:4–9; 11:13–21; and Exodus 13:1–16. Every morning (except for the Sabbath and festival days which are considered symbols in themselves) before their prayers, Jewish men put the phylacteries on their left arm and on their forehead. The Jews also wrote the commands on their door frames (*mezuzot*). In time, the singular, *mezuzah*, came to describe a long slender metal or wooden container which contains a parchment of the Deuteronomy passages already mentioned and was attached to the right door frame. When people went in or out of a house, they would put their fingers on the *mezuzah* and then on their lips as a sign of devotion for the Word which God gave to Israel. As these practices took on a more legalistic expression, the true spirit of Moses' instruction was lost. The Word of God must guide one to go beyond mere outward form; one should have the inner experience of a heart of love for the commandments and a desire to live them.

### 3. Regard for the Promised Land (6:10–25)

In Scripture, God constantly called on His people to remember His great saving acts and consider His power, love, and accomplishments for Israel in the past. On the basis of His great and mighty deeds, the people were then to have full assurance in what He could accomplish for them in the future.

**a. The Lesson of Forget-Not (6:10–19).** Moses explained to Israel that when they enter the Promised Land, they will have wealth for which they had not labored, consisting of cities and houses, many wells, vineyards and olive groves, and more. For a people who recently had walked through the desert where water was a scarce commodity, the prospect of arriving in a land with everything ready for them to use would be an ideal for which they had longed. But the danger was that in the midst of newly acquired wealth, they would forget their past experiences of walking in the desert. Most important of all, the concern was that they would forget the God who made all these things possible. The point of forget-not is that people were not to revel in the enjoyment of things, but to always remember God who made possible the material things which they had in their hands. It is also a relevant message for today's believers; in our wealth and plenty we must not forget the God who has given us all things.

To forget the Lord who would help them possess the land would be to test Him. The first generation of Israelites had done this at Massah (Exod. 17:1–7; see also Deut. 9:22) when they had quarreled with Moses about water and grumbled against him for bringing them into the desert to die there. That first generation had not remembered how gracious God had been to them, taking them through the Red Sea (Sea of Reeds). He had remained faithful to the people when they needed water, but it was in a sorry context when they grumbled that they were thirsty. God could have provided water if His people had only asked. Likewise, Israel would later forget the Lord in the midst of their plenty and would end up testing and questioning what He could do.

**b. Child Training or Child Neglect (6:20–25).** Once again Moses reminds Israelite parents that sooner or later their children would ask why Israel was different from the neighbors surrounding them. Moses challenges parents to teach their children the stipulations, decrees, and laws. In a loving family relationship encouraged by the fifth commandment, a child naturally would be curious and even willing to learn what made the families of Israel distinctive from those of pagan lands.

The father was to outline and explain to his children God's saving acts for Israel in the past: 1) Israel once had been slaves to the Egyptian Pharaoh (6:21); 2) God revealed Himself in history by bringing Israel out of Egypt and helping them cross the Sea of Reeds (6:21); 3) God judged Egypt and its pharoah (6:22); 4) God was to bring Israel to a land already promised to the patriarchs (6:23); 5) God revealed Himself to Israel through His Word, the commandments, at Mount Sinai (6:24). The fathers were to challenge their children to carefully obey the revelation of God as the basis for their righteousness (6:25). We see a parallel to the Middle Eastern treaties whereby people were to be obedient to their king so that they could have his favor and blessings. In Israel, however, as we have seen in the introduction to this commentary, the Lord-King of Israel was far above the Middle Eastern kings, and what God Himself promised would be far greater than what any mere human being could provide.

### 4. Council for War (7:1–26)

After appealing to Israel to love the Lord and yield their allegiance to Him (chap. 5–6), Moses proceeds to instruct the second generation about conquering the inhabitants of Canaan. It was necessary to instruct Israel about the Canaanites, their places of worship, as well as the idols and images which they worshiped. The nations Israel faced were described as "seven nations larger and stronger than you" (7:1).

**a. Why Destroy the Canaanites (7:1–5)?** Israel faced an impressive list of nations. The Hittites, who originally came from Anatolia (now modern Turkey), migrated and settled in the land of Canaan (Ephron the Hittite, from whom Abraham bought the cave of Machpelah, lived in the vicinity of Hebron, see Gen. 23). Not much is known of the Girgashites, who are referred to in Genesis 10:16, Joshua 3:10, and Joshua 24:11; they possibly lived in the northern part of the land. The terms "Amorites" and "Canaanites" are used widely to designate various peoples, but in this passage, seem to refer to some particular (although unidentified) peoples living in the land. The Amorites possibly lived in the hill country of Judea, while the Canaanites were located farther west along the coast (Josh. 5:1; 11:3). The Perizzites, somewhat similar to the Amorites, also appeared to live in the central hill country (Josh. 11:3); outside of the Scriptures, not too much is known of the Perizzites. The Hivites (possibly also known as the Horites or the Hurrians, according to 2:12), lived in the northern part of the land (Judg. 3:3). The Jebusites controlled what would later be the city of Jerusalem and its surrounding territory and put up a stiff resistance to Joshua and Israel in the conquest of their area.[5] The city of Jebus itself was not conquered until the days of David (2 Sam. 5:6–10). Even though the list of enemies was

---

[5] See Craigie, *Deuteronomy*, p. 178 and Thompson, *Deuteronomy*, p. 128 for a discussion of the identity and location of these peoples.

impressive, Israel had the promise that her God would overthrow all these peoples (7:1–2).

Israel was not to make any treaties with these nations. Their
covenant was with the Lord God Himself and acknowledgment
of pagan gods would be an affront to Him. No mercy was to be
extended to these pagan peoples because the Lord intended to
destroy them. Many times in the battles that ensued, the Lord
instructed the people to utterly destroy a city, including its
inhabitants and all their belongings. Such action is called *herem*
in Hebrew and is rendered by the English phrases "to put under
the ban" or "devoted" (Josh. 6:21; Judg. 1:17; 20:4, 48).

Some people question why the Israelites were so brutal
with the inhabitants of the land. Today our sensibilities are
shocked by this seemingly "cruel" action. Do not overlook,
however, God's promise to Abraham that in his day the "sin of
the Amorites" had "not yet reached its full measure" (Gen.
15:16). This suggests that at a later date, the sin of the land will
become so great that God will have to judge and destroy the
people because of their horrible, evil practices. Israel was to be
God's instrument for His justice. However, if God's people did
not do as He commanded and instead became involved with
false worship and immorality, they would be led astray and be
judged as well, as is amply illustrated in the accounts of the
prophets.

One directive of the war strategy called for the total
destruction of the pagan altars, smashing the sacred pillars,
cutting down the Asherah poles (symbols of the goddess
Asherah placed on poles at the Canaanite places of worship
[Exod. 34:13] and alongside the altar of Baal [Judg. 6:25, 28]),
and burning the idols in the fire. Israelites were to keep
themselves completely separated from the Canaanites who
remained. Intermarriages were strictly forbidden; intermarriage
would lead families in Israel astray and involve them in false
pagan worship (7:3–4). God's people were instead to set
themselves apart in worship, love, and allegiance to their God.
It is likewise a tremendous lesson for believers today, that while
we mingle with the people of the world who are involved in
their ungodly practices and ways, we still maintain a separation
from these practices. In a positive sense, we are to be sensitive

to God's holiness and righteousness and walk as His people in the midst of this world.

**b. Israel Chosen for What (7:6–16)?** God instructed Israel to go to war against the pagan nations and remain totally separate from them because she was a holy and elect nation. God made a promise to be in a peculiar relationship with Abraham and his seed throughout all their generations (Gen. 17:7). The family of Abraham by now had grown to be a nation, and (whether we look at the second generation of Israelites or the Israel of today) we see that God has a word with His people, marking them as His channel to the peoples of the world (7:6). Israel was holy, set apart to God—His treasured possession (*segullah*).

There was no specific human reason why God chose Israel. Certainly they were not the most numerous of all peoples. They were the fewest compared to the peoples of the Middle East. God chose Israel purely out of His own sovereign choice; He set His love on them and made them His people. It was out of His love that God redeemed or liberated (*padah*) Israel from bondage in Egypt, displaying His might as He took His people from pharaoh's power (7:8). God remembered His promise made with the fathers (7:6–7), and as long as human history is alive, God will remember His promise to Israel and expect her to obey His commandments (7:9).

God promised Moses that if Israel would obey the laws and keep His covenant of love, He would in turn bless Israel, increase her numbers, bless the fruit of her womb, and increase greatly the crops of the land she was to conquer (7:12–16). The Mosaic covenant was conditional; God would bless the people if they would respond to the covenant of love and live His Word. And though Israel has been disobedient at times, we must ever remember that Israel is still a chosen people under the terms of the Abrahamic covenant.

In light of God's tremendous revelation to Israel, she was enjoined to destroy the pagan peoples and to have no compassion for them. If Israel did not destroy the people, these pagans would become a snare to Israel. God's people would suffer loss in every way.

**c. Remember Pharaoh (7:17–26).** As the Israelites contemplated the task ahead of them and realized the nations in the land were stronger than they were, they undoubtedly asked, "How can we drive them out?" (7:17). But God reminded this second generation that they were not to be ensnared by the same trap as their fathers at Kadesh-Barnea. Difficulties were not measured by human strength. God asked this second generation to remember what He did to Pharaoh and Egypt (7:18–19). While Pharaoh again and again resisted Moses' pleas, in the end, Pharaoh's resistance and pride were to no avail and Israel was released.

God promised to send the "hornet" who would utterly destroy the pagan nations (7:20). We are unsure of what this term actually means. Some have taken it in a literal sense, whereby swarms of hornets would greatly assist the armies of Israel in their battles against these peoples. Other interpreters have understood this term to describe the Egyptian Pharaohs who, having the hornet as their insignia, had previously broken the power of many of the city-states of these pagan peoples, before Israel arrived on the east bank.[6] Regardless of which interpretation is used, God encouraged His people, promising that He would fight on their behalf and would give them the victory.

Moses tells the people that God would not conquer the enemies all at once, but He would gradually overtake them so that the wild animals would not multiply beyond control (7:22). Unfortunately, some later Israelite tribes did become disobedient in their command to utterly destroy these peoples, and the conquest was slowed down considerably (Judg. 2:20–23). At times the presence of Israel's enemies became a test as to whether or not Israel would be obedient to the Lord's commands (Judg. 2:22).

God promised to so utterly destroy the pagan people that no one would even remember them (7:23–24). God further charged that the silver and gold used to plate and decorate the pagan idols, even though valuable, were to be put under the ban (*herem*) and utterly destroyed. The idols were detestable

---

[6]Leon Wood, *A Survey of Israel's History* (Grand Rapids: Zondervan Publishing House, 1970), p. 88ff., where there is a discussion about the dating of the Exodus and which of the pharaohs could have broken the defenses of the Canaanite city-states.

(literally, "an abominable thing," 7:25–26), and the Israelites were to have nothing to do with them. The abominable things were not even to be taken into the houses of Israel, because if they were, the people themselves would take on the taint and also be "set apart for destruction" (7:26; see also Josh. 7).

### 5. Remember the Past—Avoid its Mistakes (8:1–10:11)

Once again Moses reminds the people of God's care in guiding this second generation. A number of themes run through this portion, and specific words serve as the main point for discussion: 1) *remember* and do not *forget;* and 2) *remember* the way God worked in the *wilderness* and ever be faithful to God in the *Promised Land.*

**a. Discipline and Provision in the Wilderness (8:1–9).** Moses reminds Israel to follow the command or commandment, which serves as an all-encompassing word to define the decrees and laws. Only if they obeyed God's revelation would He bless them once they were in the land.

Moses tells the people that God had used the wilderness experience to test the real heart motives of that first generation. But instead of learning the lesson of humility, the first generation had been found lacking, and they perished in the wilderness. These experiences were to remind later generations that they should not be found lacking.

Verse 3 describes the manna—something altogether new— which God had provided for His people. A number of commentators have attempted to explain what manna was. Some scholars have suggested that manna was the sweet substance which settles on the tamarisk trees in the Sinai in the early summer. Supposedly an insect eats the tree's sap and regurgitates it on the tree bark, leaving a sticky substance which some have thought to be manna. Or, the manna could have been the sap of this tree which oozes from the bark and collects on its branches.[7] Whatever its source, manna was God's loving and miraculous way of providing food for His people; the manna continued until Israel entered into the Promised Land (Josh. 5:12). But while the nation was to learn to wait on God to

---

[7]Thompson, *Deuteronomy*, p. 135.

provide for food, even more importantly Israel was to learn to "feed on" every word which "comes from the mouth of the LORD" (8:3). Jesus Himself illustrated this truth when Satan tempted Him in the wilderness. After Jesus had fasted for forty days, Satan came and commanded Him to make bread from the stones to meet His need for physical nourishment. The Messiah resisted the temptation (Matt. 4:4; Luke 4:4), demonstrating that life itself is more than food. Doing God's will is the best experience we can have.

Moses continues and reminds the people how God had provided for His people in a miraculous way—for the forty years of their wilderness experience, their clothes did not wear out and their feet did not swell. God is more than able to care for every need (29:5; Neh. 9:21; Matt. 6:25–34). We have to remember that even as a father disciplines a son, so God disciplined His people. God is love, and His people know that spiritual lessons are often learned through periods of suffering, deprivation, and hardship. The Israelites were being trained so that when they entered the Promised Land, they could act as mature men and women of God, walking the faith life and revering Him (8:6).

Once more, the Promised Land is described in stark contrast to the desert (8:7–8; 6:10–11). In the Promised Land the people would find streams and pools of water; springs flowing from valleys and hills; abundant wheat, barley, vines, fig trees, pomegranates, olive oil, and honey. The people would find bread or food in abundance (8:9a). The land would yield not only food but also iron and copper. Ancient copper mines and smelters have been discovered in the Negev, not far north from the modern Israelite city of Eilat. Israel today has reopened Solomon's ancient copper mines in the Timna region.[8] Modern Israel is only beginning to tap its resources of minerals in the Rimmon region in the Negev hills—the same wealth promised by God in Deuteronomy.

**b. Danger Ahead: Pride and Presumption (8:10–20).** Moses warned the people that when they would enter the land of abundance, it would be easy for them to forget their years of

---

[8] Nelson Zlueck, *The Other Side of the Jordan* (New Haven: American Schools of Oriental Research, 1940), pp. 50–88.

hardship. It would be easy to forget to praise God for His goodness. It would be easy to forget His laws and decrees (8:10–11). It would be easy to forget that it had been God who had delivered and guided them.

Again the descriptions of the material blessings are tremendous: 1) abundance of food; 2) fine houses (8:12); 3) large herds and flocks; and 4) abundance of silver and gold (8:13). It was God's intention to give His people wealth beyond imagination. But the warning amidst all the wealth was that Israelites should not become proud and forget the Lord their God who had brought them out of Egyptian slavery. In a sense God was telling them, Remember your beginning. It is a good lesson today for people who have achieved and have risen to points of prominence and wealth; they, too, are not to forget their origins. God hates the proud hearts of those who forget their benefactor, thinking they themselves have acquired prominence by their own efforts (8:14). Moses reminds the Israelites to ever remember how God had led them through the vast and dreadful desert—the dry, barren land with its snakes and scorpions (8:15). He challenges them to remember their adolescent state of testing, as God had tested what was in their hearts. God's people were to continually test their motives and make sure that the Lord was first in all areas of their lives. Never were they to say that their power and strength produced their wealth (8:17–18). The nation must learn that if she dishonors or despises her covenant relationship with God, then only judgment will ensue (8:19–20). And if the rebellion becomes irreversible, then Israel could look forward to exile (28:15ff.).

c. Majestic Power—or Man's Puny Righteousness (9:1–6). The important phrase, "Hear, O Israel," appears again (9:1). A second generation, poised on the east bank of the Jordan River, had to listen to what God had to say before any battle could begin. Their ears were to be tuned in to God's voice before their eyes were to see their enemies. As they listened to Him, a better perspective of seemingly invincible enemies and their cities would emerge. When their ear and eye perspectives were in the right order, the Israelites would see the Lord their God going before them "like a devouring fire," subduing nations and annihilating them (9:3). We also have to learn the lesson of spiritual short-sightedness. As we focus our minds and hearts on God, we will realize that the giants of this world are but puny grasshoppers in His eyes.

What was God's warning to His people? Three times Moses reminds them not to entertain any notion that God would conquer the pagans in the Promised Land because of Israel's righteousness (9:4–6). No, the pagan nations would be destroyed because of their own wickedness. A first generation exhibited themselves as "a stiff-necked people," and a second generation was not to entertain any ideas that their might or righteousness was more than the Lord's majestic power and holiness.

**d. Provocation, Stubbornness, and Defeat (9:7–29).** The theme of stubbornness and provocation is further expanded as Moses rehearses the sad experiences of a first generation.

First, they had been rebellious in spite of the great miracles God wrought for them as they were released from Egypt (9:7).

Second, they had become impatient at Mount Horeb when Moses remained on the mountain for forty days and nights, eating no food and drinking no water while God gave him the Decalogue on two stone tables inscribed by His finger. But while God had been giving the great commandments on the mountain, the Israelites had become corrupt in their idolatry and immorality (9:11–12; Exod. 32). God's response had been to call them a stiff-necked people, and they stood on the verge of complete destruction (9:13–14). Moses recalls how he had come down from the mountain and had seen what had been taking place in the camp. He had thrown the tablets on the ground, breaking them into pieces (9:15–17). But Moses then had interceded and the great anger of God was turned away once the idol had been destroyed and the people had repented of their horrible deeds (9:18–21). Moses had also prayed for Aaron, who had been pushed to commit the detestable act of making the idol (9:20; Exod. 32:1–6). God's mercy is great. The high priest of a chosen people was spared from death after committing a detestable sin.

Third, that first generation had been disobedient, and at Taberah many had been burned by the Lord's fire (Num. 11:1–3). Again at Massah, when people lacked water, they had put God to the test (6:16; Exod. 17:1–7). And at Kibroth Hattaavah, the people had complained about the manna because they had grown tired of it (Num. 11:31–34).

Fourth, the most tragic of all the disobedience had been the failure at Kadesh-Barnea, when a first generation stood on the verge of entering the Promised Land but never did (9:23–24). It seemed that in every instance, as the first generation had been tested, it had neither believed God's promises nor followed His directions.

Moses, however, had interceded for the first generation. God had been ready to destroy them, but Israel's representative had stood in the gap and interceded, reminding the Lord that He was the One who had redeemed Israel from Egypt with a mighty hand, and that these very people were His inheritance (9:25–26). He had asked God to overlook the Israelites' stubbornness, their wickedness, and their sin (9:27), reminding Him of His promises to the patriarchs. And finally Moses had asked the Lord to realize how Egypt would have the last laugh at Israel's God if He should destroy Israel in the desert (9:28).

From Moses' example we can learn what it means to be an intercessor. Moses told God that if He would not forgive the sin of Israel, then he wanted his own name to be blotted out of the Book of Life (Exod. 32:31–32). Moses' words were not mere rhetoric! God listened to Moses and respected him highly. Does He listen to the prayer of intercession? Yes! Note the many examples of such prayer: Abraham (Gen. 18:23–32); Samuel (1 Sam. 8:6–9, 21–22); Elijah (1 Kings 18:36–39); Daniel (Dan. 9:1–19); and Paul (Rom. 9:3). Many times God's judgment or the forces of hell have been stayed because of the intercessory prayer of saints. The call today is for the body of Christ to forget petty differences and enter into intercessory prayer for world outreach.

**e. New Tablets and a Fresh Beginning (10:1–11).** Once a treaty was broken in the ancient Middle East, new treaty documents were prepared and the people took a new oath of allegiance. So it was with Israel. After the Israelites had confessed and had prayed for repentance and spiritual renewal (Exod. 33), the covenant was renewed (Exod. 34:1–4). In brief summary: God renewed His mercy, two new stone tablets were prepared, a new ark was made of acacia wood, and Moses went up the mountain to receive again the Decalogue (10:1–5). (References to the ark occur in only two places, here and in 31:26, even though the ark played an important role in the history of Israel. Deuteronomy is not so much concerned with the furniture of the tabernacle as it is with the covenant relationship of Israel and its God, calling for an expression of love and reverence for the Lord.)

A parenthetical note appears in verses 6–9. In the completion of the written form of Deuteronomy, Joshua or others after him may have added information about the route of the journey, from the "wells of the Jaakanites to Moserah" (in Num. 33:30–32, the order is reversed). It is not necessary that we have an exact chronology because these places could have been visited more than once on the journey. The location of these sites could be in the vicinity of Kadesh-Barnea.

The parenthetical note reports that Aaron had died and had been buried in these regions. Elsewhere he is said to have died at Mount Hor (32:50; Num. 20:22–29), "near the border of Edom." The point is that the areas are not far apart. When Aaron's son Eleazar succeeded Aaron as the priest, we note that in spite of Aaron's sin at Mount Horeb, the Aaronic priesthood had been reestablished—only because of God's grace, love, and compassion.

After Aaron's death, Israel had moved on to Gudgodah and Jotbathah, where there were streams of water. The reference marks the southern Arabah when the people had been on the verge of coming out of the wilderness.

Moses recalls how God had set apart the tribe of Levi "to carry the ark of the covenant of the LORD, to stand before the LORD to minister and to pronounce blessings in his name, as they still do today" (10:8). Levi and Simeon had been deprived of their inheritance after their detestable behavior (Gen. 34; 49:5–7), but after the Levites had stood with Moses in the rebellion at Mount Sinai (Exod. 32:26), the tribe had been assigned the sacred duties of the tabernacle, although the high priestly duties already had been given to Aaron's family within this tribe.

The last two verses of this section sum up the main theme:

the Lord had accepted Moses' intercession on behalf of Israel (10:10–11) and therefore Israel had not been destroyed. Instead God had challenged Moses to lead Israel through the wilderness to the east bank of the Jordan River and then to prepare them to enter the Promised Land.

### 6. What Does the Lord Require of You? (10:12–11:32)

After Moses described what God had done for His people, he challenges the people, bringing them to a point of personal decision (see also Exod. 19:5; Josh. 24:14; etc.). He begins, "And now, O Israel," asking what they intend to do as a response to God's goodness.

**a. How Are We to Respond (10:12–22)?** The phrase "What does the LORD your God ask [require] of you?" can be compared to Micah's question (Mic. 6:8). In either place it is the Lord's call to total obedience. God's blessings to them were dependent on their willingness to *do* and *live* His Word. James underscores a similar sentiment in the New Testament: "Do not merely listen to the word, and so deceive yourselves. Do what it says" (James 1:22).

What the Lord requires is set forth in five action verbs: 1) *fear* the Lord your God; 2) *walk* in all His ways; 3) *love* Him; 4) *serve* the Lord your God with all your heart and with all your soul; and 5) *observe* the Lord's commands and decrees . . . for your own good. These verbs occur many times in Deuteronomy (6:13ff.; 10:12, 20; 11:22; 13:4; etc.). Over and over again, God's plea to love Him is dependent on one's attitude toward Him; God's desire was for Israel to love and serve Him. The covenant relationship is not a legalistic one; the Lord wanted a heartfelt response which would be for the people's good.

Moses reminds Israel of God's majestic greatness, reaching even to the "highest heavens" (literally, "heaven of heavens") which is under His jurisdiction (10:14). In one sense, Israel was insignificant, but because God had "set his affection" on them, Israel was His servant, chosen and set apart from all the nations. John's New Testament declaration that we as believers love the Lord because He first loved us (1 John 4:19) is nothing new in Scripture; such a possibility existed already between God and His people Israel.

Moses challenges Israel to respond to God's love by circumcising their hearts and submitting to God's laws rather than continue as stiff-necked people (10:16). An uncircumcised heart is a closed one, even as ears can also be closed (Jer. 6:10); lips can also be uncircumcised (Exod. 6:12, 30), and the words from such lips reflect a heart far from the Lord. This call for circumcision throughout the Old Testament is the appeal for people to *know* the Lord (Jer. 4:4). In the New Testament, the apostle Paul succinctly put it: "A man is not a Jew if he is only one outwardly, nor is circumcision merely outward and physical. No, a man is a Jew if he is one inwardly; and circumcision is circumcision of the heart, by the Spirit, not by the written code" (Rom. 2:28–29).

Moses continues to describe God as majestic as well as impartial in His justice. In an almost hymnlike cadence, Moses declares Israel's God the "God of gods and Lord of lords, the great God, mighty and awesome, who shows no partiality and accepts no bribes" (10:17). How should Israel respond to this God when only the most minute understanding of His nature can be known? They could at least worship Him in awe and reverence.

Even as the Lord cares for the fatherless, the widow, and the alien, so also He expected the leadership of His people Israel to be concerned for the welfare of widows and orphans, providing them with food and clothing (10:18–19). In the New Testament, believers have the same responsibilities: those in need must be cared for (Rom. 12:13; 1 Cor. 16:1–2; James 1:27; 2:1–7). In so doing, we will have the greatest opportunity for sharing the gospel message.

In particular, Moses reminds Israel that God wanted them to love the aliens, remembering that they, too, had once been aliens and slaves in a foreign land (10:19). God insisted that even though a stranger did not share full civil and religious rights with the Israelites, strangers must also be respected. Believers today likewise should not look down on nonbelievers but show compassion and love for all people.

Israel was to hold fast to the truths of the covenant and live in close relationship with what God requires (10:20; see also 10:12–13). The verb "hold fast" is an interesting choice of words which particularly expresses the relationship between a man and his wife (Gen. 2:24). Even as a husband and wife hold fast to each other, so the nation was to be united to the Lord and love Him.

Moses asks the Israelites to give God all their praise because of His great and awesome wonders on their behalf (10:21–22). Already He had fulfilled what had been promised to Abraham (Gen. 15:5), multiplying the seventy people who had gone to Egypt into a nation as numerous as the stars in the sky. Even though a first generation had died in the wilderness, the promises of God remained true. The comparison "numerous as the stars in the sky" is Middle Eastern hyperbole, but it still is a sign for Israel to recognize that He enabled the nation to grow, and therefore they belonged to Him and were to serve Him with loyalty and gratitude.

**b. Again, Love and Obey (11:1–25).** Moses continues his emphasis on God's requirements and call to obedience based on a love for God within the covenant relationship. Moses lists the basis for conduct, using a number of illustrations, challenging Israel to make the right choice for their own good.

The first requirement was that Israel was to love the Lord their God, an emphasis linked to 10:12–22 when the Israelites were asked how they would respond to the Lord. Moses literally said: "You shall therefore love. . . ." Because of the personal appeal, the Israelites were to follow through in love and allegiance to meet God's requirements. This emphasis occurs only here in Deuteronomy.

To illustrate, Moses reminds Israel of three past experiences: 1) the Exodus, when the Lord delivered Israel by His mighty hand (11:2b–4); 2) God's care for Israel in the wilderness, enabling a second generation to arrive on the east bank of the Jordan River; and 3) God's action against two of the rebels within Israel—Dathan and Abiram (11:5–6).

A first generation had to be disciplined so that they would comprehend what God can do—how He can graciously care for them. No one likes discipline, but only in such circumstances do we learn how God truly cares for us (see also Prov. 3:11–12; Heb. 12:4–11).

A second requirement shifts the focus to the future

(11:8–9). Moses reminds this generation to observe all the commandments (literally, "every commandment") so that they can be courageous to possess all that God has promised to them in His land. Future generations also had to realize that their ability to live long in such a bountiful land hinged on their obedience to and love for the Lord. The promise to enjoy all the good things in the land was not automatic.

Again Moses illustrates this by reminding them that the Promised Land would not be like Egypt (11:10–11). In the rebellion of Dathan and Abiram, a first generation had complained that Moses took them out of Egypt, "a land flowing with milk and honey" (Num. 16:12–14), and instead, had led them into the wilderness. The backward look only reflected the mentality of slavery, but God wanted His people to look forward and live as free people in His land. And yet, the land of Canaan would be a bountiful land only when it could drink the rain from heaven (11:11). In Egypt the Israelites had only to plant their seed and irrigate the land,[9] but in the Promised Land, water would be scarce, with no opportunity for irrigation. The people would have to be completely dependent on the Lord to provide the rain for the land to produce in abundance. The Israelites were to be tested in their faith in order to enjoy peace and prosperity in the Promised Land (11:12).

A third requirement stated that Israel was to 1) faithfully *obey* the commands of God; 2) *love* the Lord their God; and 3) *serve* Him with all of their heart and soul. The nation had to meet these conditions to have the Lord's blessings in days ahead (11:13; see also 10:12–13).

If Israel would be obedient, God promised to provide the rain in its due season, the "autumn and spring rains" (11:14–15). The early rains come in October–November, usually in downpours, and break the summer drought, making it possible to plow the land. The later rains occur in March–April, the last rains before summer. They are absolutely necessary for fruit trees and for a final settling of the harvest. As an added blessing, rains can occur between the early and later rains and will further ensure a good water level for the land.

---

[9] See Craigie, *Deuteronomy*, pp. 209–210, for information about how Egypt was irrigated by channels from the Nile River.

Moses warns Israel not to turn to the pagan gods, Baal and Hadad, for help (11:16). The Canaanites had many prayers to their gods to make the land fertile,[10] but God's people were reminded that only the Lord makes possible the rain. If Israel did not listen, then the Lord would shut the heavens and the ground would become hard and dry (11:17). If the Israelites would continue to be deaf, then they would learn in exile that the Lord indeed is a true and living God.

God's people today should not claim promises provided only for Israel: if believers are obedient within the body of Christ, then the Lord will bring untold prosperity. God promised Israel these things so that the people would learn to give thanks for His blessings and turn to Him with all their hearts. If God's people today are blessed materially, it is only because of His grace and mercy. And yet, the responsibility is still the same, both for Israel and today's believers who have money; they are all the more responsible to the God who makes the blessings possible.

Moses again summarizes the basic commandments (11:18–25). Some people wonder why there is a continuous restatement of the commands. But we are reminded that repetition is the mother of learning: verse 18 is a repetition of 6:8; verse 19 is a repetition of 6:7 and 4:9–10; and verse 20 is a repetition of 6:9. All of these verses reemphasize the Word. The people were encouraged to be loyal to their God in order that they as well as their children would be able to live long on the land (11:21; 4:40; 6:2). The phrase "as many as the days that the heavens are above the earth" (literally, "as the days of the heavens are above the earth") suggests forever. God intended to give the Promised Land to Israel, but any sojourn in it was dependent on their obedience to Him (11:22–23; see also 6:17). Later on Israel was in exile because of disobedience, but there is always the promise that when Israel sought the Lord their God, they could return. Today, Israelis occupy much of their land, but God is preparing His people for the day when they will indeed turn to Him with all of their heart and soul (Zech. 12:10; 13:1).

---

[10]Craigie, *Deuteronomy*, pp. 210–11.

The boundaries of the land promised to Israel, provided only in a general sense in 1:7–8, are described in verse 24 in their widest limits: from the wilderness (the south) to Lebanon (the north) and from the Euphrates River in the east to the Western or Mediterranean Sea (see Gen. 15:18). None would be able to stand before Israel because God's dread and His fear would come upon Israel's enemies (11:25; see also 2:25; and 7:23–24) so that their resistance would be futile.

**c. Decisions and Decisions (11:26–32).** Moses now concludes the first part of his second address, which gives the broad principles that were to guide Israel. He reminds the people that they must constantly make the right decisions in order to enjoy God's blessings.

Moses indicates that blessings or curses will come upon Israel, depending on whether the people are obedient or disobedient. These blessings and curses are similar to those found in the Middle Eastern treaties. In some treaties, the subjects are confronted with both blessings and curses, and if they accept the terms of the treaties, then they must be responsible to make the right decisions to enjoy the blessings and avoid the curses (11:26).

According to the Middle Eastern treaties, when a king died the new leader was required to renew the king's treaty. Israel also had its treaty renewed when Joshua took over after Moses' death. Likewise, when Joshua was about to die, the elders of the land renewed the covenant.

Moses instructs the people that when they were to enter the land, God wanted them to renew the covenant by reciting the blessings and curses from Mount Gerizim and Mount Ebal. In a precise and specific order they were to proclaim the blessings from Mount Gerizim and the curses from Mount Ebal (11:29). These mountains were located across the Jordan River, west of the road. "West of the road" is an obscure phrase, but perhaps it refers to some north-south road, linking Jericho in the south and Bethshean in the north. Canaanites lived in these areas, which also included the Arabah as well as the vicinity of Gilgal (11:30). Gilgal is often referred to as "the Gilgal," suggesting a place of prominence, ruling out the Gilgal near the Jordan River. It is located instead somewhere near Shechem.[11] The details are not clear; Moses could have recorded some information he had received at some time in the past. Nevertheless, the Israelites appeared to have no difficulty locating the place, once they went beyond Jericho and Ai (Josh. 8:30–35).

Moses closes his address just as Israel was about to cross the Jordan to take possession of the land. He reminds them once more that they must give heed to all that God had revealed to them to live peacefully in this land.

## For Further Study

1. Search through the Gospels and make a list of the passages in which Jesus quotes or paraphrases the Decalogue.

2. Search through the writings of Paul and make a list of the passages in which he quotes or paraphrases the Decalogue.

3. Compare and contrast the Decalogue and the Law Code of Hammurabi.

4. Search the writings of Paul and find the various meanings of the word "law." Ask yourself: Does the word here refer to the Old Testament, the Mosaic covenant, or some oral tradition?

5. How did the New Testament Jews treat the Sabbath commandment?

6. Why is the fifth commandment called the commandment with a promise? Find examples of this promise in Exodus, Leviticus, Numbers, and Deuteronomy.

7. With the tenth commandment as a guide, explain the difference between covetousness and godly ambition.

8. Do a word study, showing why *'ehad* can be used to demonstrate composite unity of God in the Old Testament, just as the triunity of God did for the church fathers at the Council of Nicaea. Is it possible to contextualize the truth of the persons of the Godhead in Old Testament thought?

9. Show the importance of the word "love" in the relationship between God and Israel in 4:4–11:32. Does this section teach legalism? Find the parallels in the New Testament.

10. Read 4:44–11:32 to find the passages in which God tests Israel. What was His purpose for doing so?

---

[11]Thompson, *Deuteronomy*, p. 158.

11. Read 4:44–11:32 to find passages that deal with child training. What have you learned from the passages themselves as well as from the commentaries about them?

12. Study the lifestyle of the Canaanites and other peoples in the land and determine whether you think God's order to kill them was justified.

13. How does Deuteronomy's message about living with abundance speak to the misuse of wealth today in Western society?

14. What is the purpose of remembering, according to 4:44–11:32?

# Chapter 3

## The Second Address:
## The Law of God—Part Two
(Deuteronomy 12:1–28:68)

Moses' second message deals not only with laws Israel already knew, but also with the laws not given at Mount Sinai (Exod. 20:1–23:19). The second generation was privileged to have a leader who, having already provided basic laws, could apply them to the needs of a new generation (5:3). Much of what appears in part two of this second address still rings with the authority of God, even though some of the details are not applicable today.

### A. Experience Within the Covenant Faith (12:1–26:19)

The order of presentation of the basic laws in 12:1–26:19 has been difficult to ascertain, and commentators have offered a number of suggestions in an attempt to explain the arrangement. One in particular, Stephen A. Kaufman, has made an excellent contribution to the problem.[1] After peeling away extraneous and repetitive material in chapters 12–25, he finds a striking correspondence to the Decalogue of 5:7–21, stating that commandments 1 and 2 emphasize right worship (12:1–28); commandment 4 addresses the Sabbath (15:1–18; 16:1–17); commandment 5 underscores authority, derived from parental authority (16:18–20 and 17:2–13 discuss the authority of judges; 17:14–20 addresses the law of the king; 18:1–8 discusses the authority of the priesthood; and 18:14–22 defines the authority of the prophets); commandment 6 addresses homicide (19:1–13;

---

[1] Stephen A. Kaufman, "The Structure of the Deuteronomic Law," MAARAV 1/2 (1978–79), pp. 105–158.

20:1–20; 21:1–9; 22:8); commandment 7 describes adultery and forbidden mixtures (22:9–11; 22:13–23:18); and commandment 8 addresses theft (23:1–25; 24:7).

What Kaufman calls extraneous and repetitive can be divided into three basic types:[2] 1) extraneous, completely unrelated to other materials in the total context (for example, chapters 13 and 14 as well as commandment 6 in the moving of boundary lines in 19:14); 2) commandments that are displaced (for example, commandment 6 [the laws of false witness in 19:15–21] should have been in commandment 9, or for another example, the rebellious son in 21:18–21 should belong to commandment 5); and 3) a lot of repetition and scattering of related materials. However, Kaufman feels that what is repetitive and extraneous is primarily based on the Decalogue and does not disturb the basis for the specific details (12:1–26:19). According to Kaufman, however, there are a number of laws which cannot be related directly to the Decalogue, and he suggests that Moses possibly used the materials and the form related to the Middle Eastern treaty structure. But the main thesis is upheld: Israel's leader adapted the treaty structure in his second message and expounded the Decalogue.

While handling part two of Moses' second message, we will make allusions to Kaufman's suggestions but we shall also follow an outline more suitable for our purposes. Most commentators divide Moses' message into two parts: chapters 12–14, dealing with Israel's relationship to God, and chapters 15–26, dealing with the person-to-person relationships within the nations. But we will combine chapters 12–16, which deal with worship. Further divisions will be indicated.

### 1. Worship Experience (12:1–16:17)

Part Two of Moses' second message (also known as the Code) begins with an emphasis on worship, as does the Decalogue. If a person's relationship to God is right, then the relationships to other people will also be correct. Israel could only realize her true position as the people of God as she sought to first worship and glorify her divine King. Fellowship with

---

[2]Kaufman, "Structure of the Deuteronomic Law," pp. 113–14.

God in the *divine upper look* will lead to desirable and good relations in the *human outlook*.

**a. The Sanctuary God Chooses (12:1–32; Hebrew 12:1–13:1); commandments 1 and 2 (5:7–10).** The introduction to the Code of Deuteronomy is similar to the wording in 4:44–45; 5:1, and 6:1–2. Moses announces that these are the laws and decrees that are provided as a guide whereby Israel can live peacefully in the land (12:1).

Moses mentions the first of two major concerns (12:2–3). The first concern was that the nation was to have nothing to do with pagan sanctuaries and pagan worship practices, and indeed, all such shrines everywhere were to be completely destroyed. The actual sites themselves were not abhorrent to God, but He detested the kind of worship that occurred there. Therefore, the names associated with the gods and their respective sanctuaries were to be blotted out. By contrast, God announced to Israel, "You [plural] must not worship the LORD your God in their way" (12:4), suggesting the danger of creating a synthesis: worship in the Canaanite manner but using the name of the Lord as the object of devotion.

The second concern was for the place designated by the Lord Himself for proper worship, a consideration discussed in the rest of the chapter. Israel's worship was distinctive in that God would choose the place where His name would dwell (12:5). The word "dwelling" (Hebrew *leshikno*, the noun, *sheken*) appears only here in the Old Testament, perhaps underscoring the place where the tabernacle and the ark would be located.

Where might this place be? Later, in the days of David, Jerusalem became identified as the site where the temple was to be built. Until then, there would be a transition period during which the Lord would choose a number of places for worship until the time when the permanent location would be fixed. In the meanwhile, God would manifest His presence and authority over His people at these various sites.

The Israelites could then bring their burnt offerings and sacrifices to these places (12:6).[3] In addition, they were to bring

---

[3] See Louis Goldberg, *Leviticus: A Bible Study Commentary* (Grand Rapids: Zondervan Publishing House, 1980) for a fuller presentation of these offerings listed in Leviticus 1–7.

tithes, first-born animals, and special gifts through the "putting forth of your hand" (literal from the Hebrew), indicating the portion of the animal given to the priest after he had waved it before the altar (18:4; 26:2; Lev. 7:14, 32–34). These offerings to God would be from bountiful provisions because God would abundantly bless Israel. They would have every reason to rejoice in everything they desired to do (12:7), and yet all blessings and joyous occasions were dependent on the people's love and obedience to the Lord their God.

Moses again reminds this second generation of the experiences in the wilderness when their parents had been resistant to the Lord's will. But soon Israel was to cross the Jordan River, settle in the land to rest, and live in safety from all of their enemies. Rest and inheritance, however, would only be real as Israel would remember the Lord their God and worship Him in His special place.

It is also possible that God was anticipating those tragic occasions when Israel would turn away from Him, particularly after Joshua's campaigns and during the reign of some future kings. The nation was therefore warned to keep her eyes on the Lord and come to His sanctuary at the appointed times to worship. The offerings described in 12:11 are similar to 12:6, serving perhaps as a summation. If the Israelites would only be consistent in their service, then the families, servants, and Levites would have great joy. Moses mentions the Levites in particular because in times of prosperity and peace when Israel was obedient, the offerings brought to the sanctuary would provide food in abundance for the Levites who lived in the towns (literally, "within the gates") and who had no inheritance of their own.

Once more, Moses warns the people that God did not want the burnt offerings to be offered in any place, but only in those places the Lord would mark for worship (12:13–14). He wanted Israel to avoid the pain of disobedience; obedience, however, would bring blessings and favor to the nation.

Moses also explains the kinds of animals used for food, and particularly what was to happen to the blood (12:15–16). Only acceptable animals were to be killed and used for food in the towns by both ceremonially clean and unclean people (see Lev.

11). These distinctions applied only when people were not in or near the sanctuary. The only injunction was that blood of the animals was to be poured out on the ground; since blood and life are synonymous in biblical thought, people must properly respect blood (see Lev. 17).[4]

While there was freedom to eat the meat of clean animals, no one must eat the flesh of the first-born of herds and flocks or any other animal that had been set aside in a vow, freewill offering, or special gift. These were to be brought to the sanctuary where particular portions of its meat, classified as sacred, were eaten (12:17–18). Other portions were for the priests and Levites. God cared for His people and wanted them to sense that He would use what belonged to Him to care for the Levites, His servants (12:19; Lev. 7:28–34).

The instructions given in 12:15–18 are repeated for emphasis (12:20–28). As Israelites would control more and more of the land promised to them, they would live at greater distances from a sanctuary designated by God; as a result, they would not be able to attend the sacrificial feasts as often as they wished. Therefore, Moses instructs the people that in addition to gazelles and deer (12:15), they could eat food from their herds and flocks. Even though sacrifices to the Lord were offered from certain of these animals, yet in a legitimate sense some of them could also be eaten in the local settlements. Once more, Moses warns the people not to eat blood; rather, it was to be poured out on the ground. The Israelites were to be sensitive to what was right and what was condemned.

In the closing verses, Moses challenges Israel about the dangers of false religions (12:2–4, 13–14, 29–31). They were not to be enticed by them, ask how the pagans served their gods, or even imitate their practices. God called for obedience to the covenant relationship; why should Israel follow these pagans after they had been told to completely exterminate them and their worship? The tragedy is that many in Israel, even kings, adopted these detestable and horrible practices (King Ahaz, 2 Kings 16:3; 17:17; and King Manasseh, 2 Kings 21:6). But God was adamant, warning His people not to add to or take away from His Word (12:32).

---

[4]Ibid., pp. 91–92.

**b. No Rival Worship (13:1–14:2; Hebrew 13:2–14:2).** Hard on the heels of the previous injunction was the mention of the dangers Israel faced in entanglements with pagan religions and idolatry. In the Middle Eastern suzerainty treaties, the overlord demanded undivided allegiance; in the same way, the Lord wanted complete loyalty from Israel.

This chapter divides into three parts—verses 1–5; verses 6–11; and verses 12–18 (Hebrew, verses 2–6; 7–12; 13–19); each phrase begins with "if." (Similar subject material also appears in 17:2–7, but there Israel's judges must decide on the death penalty for an Israelite charged with apostasy.)

In the first part of the chapter, the false prophet is condemned for attempting to introduce some form of pagan religions into the midst of Israelite worship. A real problem existed when evil proselytizers were able to do miracles (with Satan's help) and then call on Israel to follow the pagan gods of the Middle East. At the moment that a so-called prophet uttered such words, the people were to recognize that he was a false prophet trying to break Israel's allegiance and loyalty for their true God. (Deut. 18:9–22 discusses how to test false and true prophets.)

Moses declares that 1) Israel was not to listen to these false connivers; 2) God's people were to realize that the Lord was testing them to see if they would make the right choices, and 3) the false prophets were to be put to death (13:2–3, 5). The nation was to purge out all such evil and worship the true God.

In the second part of the chapter, Moses warns against danger from family members who would try to entice their own families to worship the pagan gods. Even family ties could not stand in the way of judging errant members of families. Once more, three actions were to be taken by true believers against their own brothers, sons, daughters, wives, and friends: 1) do not yield or listen; 2) show no pity by sparing or shielding apostates; and 3) stone to death such apostates (believers within the family were to take the first action, followed by help from the community). The penalty was certainly severe (13:9–11), but it was necessary in order to preserve the covenant relationship by curbing an evil which could spread very rapidly.

Love for the Lord was even more important than love for a

family member who had gone astray. Lest the reader find such a concern too harsh, Jesus Himself said on one occasion that a true disciple must love the Lord first of all—more than father, mother, wife, children, brothers, sisters, and even his or her own life (Luke 14:26). God is not interested in anything less than total allegiance.

In the third section of the chapter, Moses warns against yet another danger. If the people were to learn that a number of wicked men ("worthless men") in any of the towns were enticing people to practice idolatry (13:12–18), the evil people were to be dealt with in a certain way. To avoid any miscarriage of justice in case the report was not entirely true, the report had to be investigated thoroughly. If the people verified that a "detestable thing" (a word used in the Old Testament to describe what is absolutely displeasing to God, see also 7:25–26; 14:3; 17:1, 4; 18:9; 20:18) had been committed within Israel, then they were to put to death all who live in the town, destroying it completely, both people and livestock. The term "destroy it completely" refers to what is given over totally to the Lord. Everything was to be gathered together in the public square of the town, and both plunder and town were to be burned, as a burnt offering to the Lord (13:16). Is this too harsh? Again, one must realize that a nation's total consecration to the Lord and her allegiance to Him was at stake. If apostasy and rebellion broke out, they had to be punished; nothing less could reflect the holiness of God (Num. 25:4–9; Josh. 6:17–21).

The point is emphasized further. In view of Israel's high calling, she was not to become involved in the many pagan practices. The people were not to cut their bodies or shave their heads (14:1). These were Middle Eastern pagan rites for mourning (mentioned in Isa. 3:24; Jer. 16:6; Ezek. 7:18; Amos 8:10; Mic. 1:16). Israelites were to have respect for their bodies that God created, and they were not to be disfigured (Lev. 19:27–28; 21:17–21). Even a priest had to be very careful about physical defilement (Lev. 22:3–8). These rites might also encourage contact with the dead through pagan occult media and these, too, were strictly forbidden (18:11). In order to curb unnecessary physical contact with the dead, the law declared that anyone who touched a dead body was considered ritually unclean (Num. 19:11–18; 31:19).

**c. What Shall We Eat (14:3–21)?** Offhand, one might wonder why instructions regarding foods had anything to do with worship. But for a number of reasons, what Israelites ate was very clearly a part of their regard for the Lord their God.

God gave the Israelites strict dietary laws for several reasons. Hygiene was very important, and toxicity in some of the animals, fish, and birds could be deadly (Lev. 11).[5] Also, certain foods were to be avoided because of their religious connotation:[6] the pig was a sacred animal to the god Baal at Ugarit; some fish were worshiped in Egypt; and certain birds (the crow or raven) were on the standard or totem for certain Arab families.

Another basic reason for strict dietary laws was the concern for blood.[7] Most of the animals and birds that were considered unclean are predatory, eating both flesh and blood. Israelites were to respect the blood of any life form and were instructed, therefore, to avoid those life forms which eat the blood of other life forms.

The basic reason for the dietary laws was a theological one, but perhaps one can see the validity of the other two as well. Any food that was forbidden was regarded as a "detestable thing" (14:3).

Animals regarded as clean were those that chewed the cud and had split hoofs (14:4–6). Those animals that met only one of the requirements—camels, rabbits, rock badgers, and pigs— were forbidden (14:7–8). In particular, the pig is unclean: it eats all kinds of garbage, and if the flesh is not cooked properly, one can get trichinosis. Fish which have both fins and scales were appropriate for food. All other marine creatures were strictly forbidden (14:9–10). Lobsters and crabs were very dangerous; to prepare them properly for food, one must drop them live into boiling water. When they are killed otherwise, a poison is released into their flesh, causing serious health problems to those who eat them.

Fowl that were forbidden were those that are carnivorous, eating flesh and blood (14:11–18). Flying insects were carefully defined: crickets, locusts, and grasshoppers with two strong back

[5]Craigie, *Deuteronomy*, p. 230.
[6]Ibid., *Deuteronomy*, p. 230 and Thompson, *Deuteronomy*, p. 178.
[7]See Goldberg, *Leviticus*, pp. 65–66.

legs for leaping were permitted for food (Lev. 11:21–22), but all other flying insects were to be avoided because they eat flesh and blood (14:19).

Finally, the Israelites were not allowed to eat the corpse of any animal that had died of natural causes. Again the blood is important, especially if the corpse did not have the blood released from it in the proper manner (12:23). Touching dead animals made a person ritually unclean, and the Israelites were to remember that they were a people holy to the Lord their God. They were not to violate His guidelines for proper eating so they would live with healthy bodies; they could give dead animals to aliens living among them, or they could sell them to foreigners (14:21). By obeying the Lord, Israel would be able to share God's Word with the foreigners and even bring them to saving faith.

The law regarding cooking a young goat in its mother's milk (14:21; Exod. 23:19; 34:26) was a Canaanite rite and is described in a Ugarit text.[8] The pagans cooked the kid in the milk, a lamb in the cream, and then took the broth and poured it out on their fields to insure good crops. The Israelites were to understand that if they were faithful to their God, He would cause the rains to fall and make the Promised Land fertile. In the religious customs of later Judaism, this injunction was and is applied to separating meat and dairy products. Orthodox Jews observe this injunction to this day.

**d. The Joy of Giving (14:22–29).** One might wonder why the subject of tithing appears in the midst of a discussion of how Israel was to worship the Lord God. Giving, however, is an experience of worship.

The language of the verb is emphatic, "Be sure" to tithe (14:22). The Israelites were not to tithe in a legalistic sense, thinking that by bargaining with God, they could gain His blessing. The spirit of genuine giving is to give out of a joyous heart because of all the blessings God will make possible. In the New Testament, some of the religious leaders were rebuked because, even though they gave the tithe, they neglected the more important matters of the law (Matt. 23:23; Luke 11:42;

---

[8]Thompson, *Deuteronomy*, p. 179.

18:12). Paul reminded believers to give generously to the work of the Lord, to go even beyond the tithe because "God loves a cheerful giver" (2 Cor. 9:7).

A comparison of Leviticus, Numbers, and Deuteronomy reveals different instructions for tithing. In Numbers 18:21–28, the entire tithe is given to the Levites, and in turn, the Levites pay their tithes to the priests. In Deuteronomy, part of the tithe is to be spent at the sacred feasts at which the offerer and his household partake, and the rest is set aside for the relief of the poor. In both situations, the Levite shares only in company with others.

In addition, Deuteronomy specifies that the tithe be taken from what is produced in the field (although mention is made also of the tithe of wine, oil, herds, and flocks). Numbers 18:27–30 suggests a tithe of what grows in the fields and vineyards. Leviticus 27:30 mentions the tithe of the field as well as the herd and flock.

During the intertestamental period, Jewish religious leaders attempted to reconcile these principle passages. In Tobit 1:7, in Josephus' *Antiquities of the Jews* (iv.8.22), and in later materials, the Deuteronomy passages do not refer at all to the tithe mentioned in Leviticus and Numbers. Rather, Deuteronomy mentions a second or additional tithe to be gathered—after giving the Levitical tithe—on the remaining nine-tenths of the produce of the fields. This second tithe was used not only in public festivals which took place at the sanctuary but also to provide for the poor, which was considered a third tithe.[9]

How are we to reconcile the biblical passages? The differences between the passages are not that serious, although there does appear to be some variation in the detail. As Moses expounded and interpreted the instructions for tithing, he told the people to use the *entire* tithe for some communion feast at the sanctuary (14:23–27). If Israelites lived too far from the sanctuary, they could sell their produce and animals for silver, which was then brought to the sanctuary. They could then buy cattle, sheep, or wine near the sanctuary and join in the worship and communion fellowship. One commentator suggests that

---

[9] S. R. Driver, *Deuteronomy* in *The International Critical Commentary*, 3rd ed. (Edinburgh: T. & T. Clark, 1902), pp. 169–70.

since such a huge quantity of food would be consumed, perhaps only a portion of the money was used for the communion feast, while the rest was given to the Levites who then paid their tithe of it to the priests and kept the rest for themselves.[10] This communion fellowship at the central sanctuary took place on the first, second, fourth, and fifth years of the Sabbatical cycle. On the third and sixth years, the entire tithe was to be kept locally and used for the care of the poor.

The Israelites were to take their tithe from the grain, new wine, and oil of the olive trees. Also included were the firstborn of the herds and the flocks. While the law of the tithe is not presented in a precise manner, Moses did mention the importance of tithing, making sure that it would be used for what the Lord intended. The directives to bring the tithe to the sanctuary were also insurance that Israelites would not turn to the pagan sanctuaries and take their tithes to those detestable places. Instead, the communion festivals were opportunities for God's people to rejoice in the presence of the Lord their God.

The meal at the sanctuary consisted of the herds and flocks, wine and fermented drink (intoxicating, *shekar*), but in no way were people to become drunk at these communion festivals. Every third year, the tithe was to be kept locally, stored in each town, and used for the needy. Each Israelite was to make a statement that his tithe had been offered (26:13–15). The instructions for tithing closed with the exhortation that as the poor are cared for, then the Lord, the God of Israel, will bless them in all the work of their hands (14:29). God's people, those of both the Old and New Testaments, were ever to keep in mind that compassion must be extended to those in desperate need (Deut. 24:15; Prov. 22:22–23; James. 1:27).

**e. Covenant Faith and Release From Debt (15:1–11); commandment 4 (5:12–15).** As Moses enunciates the principles of the law and its reflection of Israel's completely righteous God, he expresses God's concern for the rights of every person, whether rich or poor. While the Code of Hammurabi describes how the king sought to rectify all injustices, particularly in the

---

[10]Thompson, *Deuteronomy*, p. 182.

first year of reign, the high ranking people of the society had a definite advantage over the poor and the needy.[11] In the Code of Deuteronomy, by contrast, Israel's righteous Judge made no distinction between the rich and the poor; many times God became the champion of the needy.

Moses explains to Israel that at the end of seven years, all debts were to be canceled or released. The word "release" (from the Hebrew *shemittah*) literally means "letting go." This term is also used in Leviticus 25:33ff. as a directive to let the land rest every seventh year within a jubilee cycle of fifty years. During this Sabbatical year then, every creditor was to release all loans made to fellow Israelites because God intended all debts to be canceled. The law gave the poor every opportunity to have a fresh start with their economic responsibilities. The idea of release reflects commandment 4 and applies not only to the day of rest, but also to rest for the land every seven years and relief from the burden of a crushing load of debt. The Jewish Publication Society's translation of Deuteronomy 15:1–2 provides an alternative understanding whereby only the interest on a loan was remitted in the Sabbatical year: "Every creditor shall remit the due that he claims from his neighbor; he shall not dun his neighbor or kinsman."

Moses gives additional instructions for remission of debts (15:3–11). A distinction was made between an Israelite and the alien as well as the foreigner. The alien, although not a member of the state, came under the law of remission. But since foreigners were transient, they were liable for all their debts.

God promised prosperity to the people of Israel if they would fully obey the Lord their God and follow all of His commands (15:4–6). No similar promise of material prosperity can be carried over into the church because God promises only to care for our needs (Phil. 4:19). But Israel was constituted as a nation, living on a selected land provided for them by the Lord. If the people were completely loyal to their God, He would bless so abundantly that there would be no poor in the land, and therefore no need for a year of release. Everyone would have more than enough. Unfortunately, when the unbelievers re-

---

[11] Ibid., p. 185.

belled against the Lord, He had to judge them by withholding rain, creating a hardship not only for the rebels but also for the innocent poor (28:15ff.).

Moses tells the people that whoever had the means was to give generously to a fellow Israelite, even as God was patient and generous with His people Israel. In fact, one should go beyond merely forgiving debts every seventh year and provide help any time it was needed (15:7–8).

Moses warns about creditors who, because the need for help was so near to the Sabbatical, might be stingy and show ill will (literally, "your eye is hostile") to the needy and not make the loan (15:9). Moses makes clear that God will condemn such an attitude and judge the evil creditor; God is the champion of the poor and needy. The New Testament echoes the same challenge for people to be generous and compassionate (Matt. 6:1–4; Luke 14:12–14), reflecting godly priorities and motives (1 John 3:17).

**f. The Slave Can Go Free (15:12–18).** Another reflection of commandment 4, with its emphasis on rest, was the release of the Hebrew servant. When a person became so poor that he or she was not able to pay debts before the Sabbatical, that person entered into a work contract with a wealthy Israelite to pay off his debts. After six years of service—not the six years of the Sabbatical cycle—the servant was freed (15:12).[12] The term "fellow Hebrew" (literally, "brother") is used to describe the Israelite servant (15:12) as a member of the household of Israel which was really one big family. Everyone within that society was therefore equal before God; the poor and the servants were not to be degraded.

When the Israelite servant was finally free, he or she was not to be sent away empty-handed. An Israelite master was to give to a freed servant liberally of flocks, grain, wine, and oil so the servant would have enough to begin life with a new start. This kind of sharing was based on love and compassion for the poor (15:7–11). Moses instructs the people that through the act of freeing a servant, the Israelites were to remember that they, too, once had been slaves, and a gracious and merciful God had freed them and placed them in the Land of Promise (15:14–15).

---

[12] Craigie, *Deuteronomy*, p. 238.

On occasion, a Hebrew servant preferred to remain a life-long servant. Such a choice might be strange to us today, but it was not strange in the country where life was difficult and where a servant could also have a trusted position in the family he or she served (15:16). When a servant chose this life, a special religious and civil ceremony marked his or her new status. The servant was to stand before the judges (in a sense, God) and the servant's earlobe was placed on the doorpost and was bored through with a pin into the post (15:17). The ear was the symbol of obedience (Ps. 40:6), and so the servant was to serve the master's family. Such a person became a "servant for life," (15:17), a phrase that also appears in the Ugarit literature.[13]

Moses warns masters not to balk at freeing a servant. Even though the servant did not work for wages, the six years of service were considered twice as much as that of a hired servant and were considered full payment on the debts. Perhaps the word "twice" is seen in the light of the Code of Hammurabi, where a servant only served for three years.[14]

**g. The First-born Is Sacred to the Lord (15:19–23).** All first-born animals were to be regarded as sacred to the Lord (12:6, 17; 14:23), but a further distinction is also made between perfect and imperfect animals. The perfect first-born animals were to be sacrificed to the Lord, while the others could be used for ordinary purposes.

The first-born of all animals were to be treated differently from all other animals. First-born oxen were not to be worked, and first-born sheep were not to be sheared in order to benefit from them (15:19). Such perfect first-born creatures were offered to the Lord, and their flesh was to be eaten in communal celebration (14:23) at the time when families also brought their tithes to the sanctuary chosen by God (15:20). The first-born animals that had defects, however, could be slaughtered and eaten at home, much like animals taken as game (12:15, 22). Anyone who offered blemished animals to the Lord was flouting His holiness; furthermore, since animal sacrifices were symbols or types that point toward the Messiah to come, the lesson of the anti-type would also be destroyed (15:21–22).

---

[13] Ibid., p. 239.
[14] Ibid., p. 239.

Finally, Moses instructs the people that when they slaughtered the first-born animals, they must be careful with the blood,
ever keeping in mind its sacredness because it was synonymous
with life (12:16).

**h. Celebrating the Holidays (16:1–17).** Moses continues his
instructions by explaining how Israel was to observe three
special occasions: 1) Passover and Unleavened Bread, 2) the
Feast of Weeks (Pentecost), and 3) the Feast of Tabernacles.
These festivals were also agricultural observances; two of them
pointed specifically to the events which marked the time of the
Exodus from Egypt.

**(1) Passover, From the Hebrew *Pesah* (16:1–8).** Israel was
to observe the Passover during the month of Abib (16:1). The
word "month" means the new moon, and Abib (literally, "the
month of the green ears") occurs during March–April. (The
Canaanite calendar was the one used in the pre-exile period.
Later, during and after the Babylonian exile, Israel adopted the
Babylonian calendar and this month was renamed Nisan.)
Because Abib came in the springtime, it marked the spring
festival, but this particular month took on new historical
significance at the time of the Exodus when the Lord delivered
Israel from Egypt.

On the occasion of this festival, people were to sacrifice a
passover animal (16:2). The Hebrew word used here is *pesah*,
the same word used to describe the holiday in 16:1. The choice
of animals from the flock or the herd is interesting, because
during the first Passover, a lamb was specified as the sacrificial
animal (Exod. 12:3–5). Keil and Delitzsch suggest that Moses
had in mind all the animals sacrificed during the Passover and
Feast of Unleavened Bread but only a lamb was sacrificed for
the Passover itself.[15] Craigie thought that Moses suggested that,
since two-and-a-half tribes were already on their land which was
wealthy in cattle, it would be all right to offer animals from the
herd and flock for the Passover sacrifice.[16] In the days of the
New Testament, Judaism prescribed that only lambs could be
offered for the Passover.

[15] C. F. Keil and F. Delitzsch, *The Pentateuch,* Vol. III, in the *Biblical Commentary on the Old Testament,* tr. James Martin, (Grand Rapids: Wm. B. Eerdmans Publishing Company, 1951), pp. 374–75.
[16] Craigie, *Deuteronomy,* p. 242.

Originally, each family had observed the first Passover at home and had sprinkled the blood of the animals on the lintels and doorposts to protect their first-born from the death angel. Once Israel was in its land, the celebration of Passover was to be in the place which the Lord designated as His dwelling. (When the second temple was destroyed in A.D. 70, the practice of Passover again became a home festival.)

The Feast of Unleavened Bread (*maṣot*) was related to the Passover (Exod. 23:14–17), and in the seven days following Passover, only unleavened bread was to be eaten (16:3–4; Exod. 12:14–15; Lev. 23:5–6).

The history of the Exodus was to become a part of the national consciousness. As the Passover was enacted every year in a Passover dinner (from the Hebrew *seder*, meaning "order"), Israel reminisced what occurred when God had delivered her from Egypt. The unleavened bread itself was a reminder of the hardships Jewish people endured in Egypt.

During the Feast of Unleavened Bread, the firstfruits of the barley were also offered to the Lord, marking this festival as an agricultural one as well. No matter where the people of Israel have wandered in the centuries after the first century, their minds and hearts have been reminded not only of the religious emphasis of this particular holiday, but also of their homeland because of the agricultural significance of the barley harvest.

During the celebration of the Passover and Unleavened Bread, leavened bread was prohibited at the sanctuary and everywhere else in the land during the seven days (16:4; Exod. 12:14–20; 13:3, 6–7; 34:18; Lev. 23:6). In addition, the meat of the sacrifice eaten in the evening of the first day of the festival was not to be left over until morning (Exod. 12:10; 23:18b; 34:25b; Num. 9:12). Leaven and stale meat were signs of impurity.

The Passover animal was sacrificed in late afternoon, as the sun was going down, a reminder that the Exodus took place in the evening (16:6). After the priests received their share of the sacrifice, the rest was to be roasted in the fire and then eaten in the area of the sanctuary (16:7; Exod. 12:8–9). Never was it to be eaten raw or boiled. The morning after eating the Passover, the people could return to their tents. In later urban situations,

Israelite pilgrims came to the temple in Jerusalem from afar, and many of the people in the city provided for and made them welcome in their homes, although in most situations, people had to have accommodations outside of the city walls.[17] In New Testament times, as many as one million people visited Jerusalem during Passover, and the seventh day was a day of assembly, when no work was done (Num. 28:18).

(2) Feast of Weeks (16:9–12). The second of the major festivals was identified by a number of names: Feast of Harvest (Exod. 23:16), and the Day of Firstfruits (Num. 28:26); Pentecost was used in the Septuagint (Greek translation of the Old Testament) because of the translation of Leviticus 23:16 which describes how this holiday is determined. The Feast of Weeks marked the wheat harvest on the agricultural calendar.

The holiday is dated seven weeks plus one day (fifty days) after the sickle was put to the standing barley grain (Lev. 23:15–16). Fifty days approximated the time from the beginning of the barley harvest to the end of the wheat harvest. While there were variations of the harvest in different parts of the land, Moses fixed the dates so that the holiday could be observed by everyone at the same time. Since the second of these festivals is also an agricultural one, no matter where Jewish people were in their exiles, they would ever remember another harvest in the land and could not forget their attachment to it.

Both Jewish and church calendars are providentially linked: 1) even as the firstfruits of the barley harvest were offered up at the beginning of the Passover season, so Jesus in His death during this season was offered up as a firstfruit of the body of believers to follow; and 2) even as the firstfruits of the wheat harvest were offered up some fifty days later, so the 3,000 who became believers on Pentecost were the firstfruits of the general harvest of souls yet to come into the body of Christ.

When people came to the central sanctuary to observe the Feast of Weeks, they had to bring a freewill offering, a gift, in proportion to the Lord's blessing (16:10). Obviously it was an offering over and above the fixed daily and Sabbath offerings.

---

[17] Alfred Edersheim, *The Temple, Its Ministry and Services at the Time of Jesus Christ* (Grand Rapids: Wm. B. Eerdmans Publishing Company, 1951), p. 184.

Worshipers were to rejoice as they took part in a communion festival of the good things of God. Those who participated included not only parents and their sons and daughters, but also servants, Levites, aliens, orphans, and widows. Israel was to remember the years of slavery in Egypt (16:12), and therefore, servants and aliens were to be treated kindly and were to be invited to share in the feast (15:15; 24:18, 22).

(3) **Feast of Tabernacles (16:13–17).** The third feast, the greatest of all, also had a variety of names: the Feast of the LORD (Lev. 23:39), the Feast (Ezek. 45:25), and Feast of Ingathering (Exod. 23:16; 34:22). Tabernacles was also a harvest festival, marking thanksgiving time (Lev. 23:40), and is the general harvest of the land, occurring in either September or October. The grapes and other fruits ripened in late summer and were already harvested by the time of the feast. Jewish people could neither forget this holiday nor its attachment to the land throughout all their wanderings.

Tabernacles was celebrated for seven days, from the fifteenth day of the seventh month until the twenty-first day (Lev. 23:33). When this feast occurred during the Sabbatical year, the law was to be read to all Israel gathered at the central sanctuary (31:9–13). In the New Testament, the Gospel of John records how Jesus used the occasion of the seventh day of the Feast of Tabernacles to announce that He Himself was the messianic fulfillment of this festival (John 7:37–39). On the twenty-second day of the month, the eighth day of the festival, there was to be a convocation, a special day set apart to commemorate the closing of all the three pilgrimage festivals (Lev. 23:36) as a joyous occasion for everyone in the community.

Verses 16–17 give Moses' summary of the great lessons of the pilgrimage festivals. Here again we find a parallel to the suzerainty treaties. In the Middle Eastern treaties, the subjects were instructed to appear periodically before the king to proclaim their loyalty and bring him gifts. Similarly, the Israelites were to appear before their King and honor Him for what He provided. Although Passover is not mentioned, it is included in the Feast of Unleavened Bread (16:16; Exod. 23:14–17; 34:23).

## 2. Guidelines for a Godly Lifestyle and the Affairs of State (16:18–25:19).

Israel was a theocracy with the Lord as their God and King. The covenant provided for a unique blend of civil and religious law which would guide in decisions affecting political, judicial, and religious spheres. In the early days until the kings were established, Israel was a loose confederacy governed by judges who were regents of God. Later the kings acted in that capacity. But whatever political leadership was in authority, the people of Israel were never to forget that they were not like all other nations; rather, God was to be their true King.

**a. The Judges (16:18–20); commandment 5, with its emphasis on authority. (5:16).** Even as children were to be subject to parental authority, so the people Israel were to be subject to the authority of the officials of the state. All of them in a sense were to be responsible to the Lord and serve Him. Judges and officials were to be appointed for each tribe in every town (16:18). The judges may have functioned as our modern judges do, while the officials were the ones who were to carry out the decisions of the judges. During the Exodus and in the desert, Moses acted as the chief judge, with representatives of the various tribes serving as his assistants (1:12–18; Exod. 18:13–27). Later the priests were the ones to provide authentic interpretation of the law and act as judges (Mal. 2:7), but on many occasions judges were also chosen from other tribes. At times the local councils of each town served as judges (19:12).

Local judges were the first ones to gather evidence and issue decisions in legal cases. Where it was difficult to ascertain a solution, these cases were then sent to the judges at the central sanctuary (17:8).

Three basic rules were laid down to guarantee a true decision (16:19; Exod. 23:1–3, 6–9): 1) no one was to pervert justice; 2) justice must be impartial; and 3) no judge should ever take bribes. Bribe taking blinded the eyes of the leaders and perverted justice. God promised to condemn judges who twisted or perverted the words of the righteous (27:19). The Israelites were to follow justice and only by doing so could they live long in the land and experience the blessings of the Lord. These are the very same principles which must be followed in our court systems today if we are to be blessed as a nation.

**b. Careful Investigation of Offenders (16:21–17:7).** Offhand, one might wonder why the practice of idolatry is included in this discussion of judges and righteous judgment. But there is a significant interrelationship between religious practices and judicial procedures within the theocracy. When reports of wrongdoing reached the judges, they had to carefully investigate the accuracy of such reports before dispensing justice (13:1–18). Deuteronomy mentions three cases which necessitated investigation by the judges: idolatry, offering defective animals to the Lord, and apostasy.

In the case of idolatry, the Israelite was strongly advised not to become entangled with the false worship of the Asherah or Baal worship of the pagans of the land, or even mix pagan worship with the worship of the Lord (16:22). Tragically, there were a number of occasions of false worship even in the temple itself (2 Kings 23:6; Ezek. 8). The Lord is the God of Israel, and in cases of a perversion of true worship, judges were to examine the evidence and execute swift judgment if the charges were true. If they did not, then God Himself would have to take matters into His own hands.

Still another evil was the offerings of defective animals, either as firstfruits (15:19–23) or in any other sacrifice to God. Such a situation occurred in the days of Malachi when he charged such offenders of despising the name of God (Mal. 1:6–8). The judges had to uphold the honor of the Lord and execute His justice against offenders.

Apostasy (17:2–7; 4:15–24; 13:1–18) violated the covenant because it is contrary to God's direct command not to worship the false gods or the gods of sun, moon, or stars of the sky. Two valid witnesses against the accused would be enough for judges to investigate the charges. If after thorough investigation the judges found the charges to be true, then offenders were to be stoned to death outside of the camp (17:5). Lest people today think that such justice was hideous, let us never forget that Israel's God is holy and righteous, and rival worship is an affront to His very person.

**c. The Central Tribunal (17:8–13).** Cases too difficult for decisions at the local level were sent on to the higher court in an attempt to secure a just decision. But once a decision was rendered at the central tribunal, no higher appeal was possible. The judges at the highest level spoke as from God.

Some cases were too difficult to resolve (17:8): 1) deciding whether a person had committed premeditated murder or manslaughter (19:1–13; Exod. 21:12–14); 2) cases of lawsuits over property where the rights of the victim needed to be upheld and the offender must make restitution; and 3) cases of assault or personal injury (Exod. 21:12–34).[18]

The central tribunal was made up of priests and judges in office at the time of the inquiry. Later Jehoshaphat set up a court comprised of Levites, priests, and certain laymen (2 Chron. 19:5–11). The high priest acted as the president of the court when questions of a religious nature were considered while a layman was the chief of the court when secular affairs were taken up. After the second exile, the same procedure was followed, and in New Testament times, each town and city had its Sanhedrin which rendered decisions on the local level. But a national Sanhedrin in Jerusalem, over which the high priest presided, considered difficult cases referred to them.

The judges of the high court were to be astute and experienced in order to render righteous decisions in hard-to-resolve cases. Once the verdict was given, the persons involved had to obey the decision and not turn away from it, either to the right or to the left. Rebelling against the court's ruling was seen as rebellion against the Lord, and such a perverted person was put to death (17:12). People were to respect and revere the decisions of the high court.

**d. The King of God's Choice (17:14–20).** The second generation in Moses' day was still considered a tribal confederacy and would remain so for some time once the land had been conquered. Eventually, the nation would be sufficiently urbanized, necessitating a more centralized government, and instructions were provided for establishing a king who was to serve as the principle regent under the true King.

---

[18]Thompson, *Deuteronomy*, p. 202.

Israel was already a theocratic kingdom when the Mosaic covenant was ratified (Exod. 19:6), but in time the Lord would choose who would be king. He had to be an Israelite and not a foreigner (17:15). Once chosen, he had to be sensitive to three prohibitions: 1) He must not acquire multitudes of horses. (Egypt was a likely place to obtain horses; there was a danger that many Israelites might return there for lucrative horse trading and other business ventures). 2) He must not take many wives. Many times in the conclusion of trade treaties between nations, women were given as wives. Should an Israelite king acquire pagan wives, they could bring their idolatrous practices into the highest ranks of the nation, thereby enticing Israelites away from the Lord's worship. And 3) he must not pile up gold and silver (17:16–17). The nations of Moses' day built their military might on great quantities of horses and multiplied harems and fortunes. But Israel was not to be like other nations.

Israel's king was to have a copy of the law and to continually read it. Note another parallel to the treaties of the ancient Middle East where these treaties were periodically read in public as a reminder to the subjects to be obedient to their king. The law was also deposited with the Levitical priests, and one of their functions was to present the king with a copy for his study. With the knowledge of the will of God for governing the nation, the king could avoid all of the temptations of the nations around him (see 2 Kings 11:12).

Whenever the kings were obedient to these instructions, they enjoyed the blessings of the covenant. But when leaders did not follow the Word, they and their children suffered the judgment of God. Furthermore, no king was to consider himself better than his brothers, because all Israelites, whether officials or lay people, were equal in God's eyes (17:20). But the king had to realize that he was responsible for the nation as the regent for the true King.

**e. The Priests, the Religious Leaders of the Nation (18:1–8).** Deuteronomy makes it clear that within the entire tribe of Levi, the priests were a smaller group who were assigned the function of ministry, including the offering of the sacrifices. But the tribe had many duties apart from the priests as well, including helping the priests and taking care of the sanctuary. Nevertheless, the entire tribe did have the function of teaching the law to Israel (33:10a; Lev. 10:11; 2 Chron. 15:3; 17:8–9; 30:22).

When Jacob blessed the tribes, Levi and Simeon were actually cursed and could therefore receive no land (Gen. 49:5–7). Later when the Levites came to Moses' aid during the rebellion at Mount Horeb (Exod. 32:28–29), they demonstrated their interest in the Lord's purposes. God, therefore, made it possible for this tribe to have an inheritance by serving Him. Even though they could own no land, the Levites could live in towns (Josh. 21) and own plots of land through the sale and purchase of family property (18:8; Jer. 32:7ff.). They were, however, dependent on the offerings made by fire and whatever else was stipulated in the law (18:5; Lev. 2:3; 7:6–10; Num. 18:9ff.). The priests also shared in the firstfruits of the grain, new wine and oil, and the first wool from the sheep shearing (18:4).

There appear to be some differences between what is allowed as offerings in Leviticus 7:28–36 and Numbers 18:8–19 and what is allowed according to 18:3. In the other two books, the breast of the thanksgiving or peace offerings were to belong to all of the priests, while each officiating priest could have the right thigh of the peace offering (Lev. 7:32). Deuteronomy states that the shoulder, the two jowls (cheeks), and the inner parts (stomach) were the priests, but Moses certainly had the right to interpret the law, making it possible for the priests to have sufficient food.

Care was also taken to allow for future contingencies when priests, living in various towns, might decide to come to the central sanctuary to minister and reside (18:6–8). No vested interests therefore were to limit him from his ministry or what he could receive for food. The Levites, along with all who were needy and poor, were dependent on the tithe of the poor and the generosity of compassionate people (12:12, 19; 14:27; 16:11), and even though a particular Levite might have some private source of income, he still shared equally in the benefits with the rest of God's servants.

**f. Diviners or Prophets of God (18:9–22).** The prophets were also leaders of the state. Israel was considered a theocracy, and those who spoke on behalf of God in a legitimate sense were considered His representatives. Moses first describes the false prophets and then defines legitimate prophets.

**(1) False Prophets (18:9–14).** When Israel would conquer
the land, they were not to learn the detestable practices and
ways of the pagan nations; no other powers were to be
acknowledged apart from the Lord. Israel was to avoid the
abominable practices of the pagans and the devices of the false
prophets.[19]

One horrible practice was to make children pass through
the fire. Perhaps some magical benefit was derived from it, such
as attempting to alter the course of future events. The religious
practice appeared to be associated with the god Molech
(2 Kings 23:10; Jer. 32:35) and acknowledged by the Moabites
(2 Kings 3:26–27).

Moses mentions four occult practices (18:10): 1) divina-
tion—attempting to discern the will of the pagan gods (Nebu-
chadnezzar used it by whirling his arrows, seeking to determine
the will of the gods by exactly how the first arrow came out of
the holder; Ezek. 21:21); 2) sorcery—determining the will of
the gods by reading the formation of the clouds or by various
incantations; 3) omens—attempting to divine the will of the
gods by the way light was reflected from the surface of the liquid
in a cup (Gen. 44:5, 15; although it is doubtful that Joseph made
use of it); and 4) witchcraft—determining information by using
certain types of herbs for magical purposes (Mic. 5:12).

Moses continues his catalogue of detestable practices.
Casting spells was practiced in the attempt to control people,
binding them by a spell (18:11; Ps. 58:5a). Mediums were those
persons who would inquire of a ghost or spirit who then would
speak from within the person (Lev. 20:27). At times, the medium
attempted, and on some occasions even succeeded to call up the
spirits (1 Sam. 28:11). Spiritists were those persons who con-
sulted spirits for information. Finally Moses mentions those who
consult or call up the dead, actually calling on spirits or dealing
with a familiar spirit (Isa. 8:19).

All of these pagan practices were detestable to the Lord
(18:12). False worship was nothing less than communicating
with Satan and his kingdom, and Israel was to steer clear of it
and be blameless before God (18:13). Moses' instructions are

[19]Ibid., pp. 210–12.

still valid today. Believers should have absolutely nothing to do with the occult; believers should rely only on what God has revealed in His Word.

(2) **Genuine Prophets (18:15–22).** By contrast, the Lord was to give Israel genuine prophets who would share His message with the nation. Tests were provided to ascertain the credentials of a genuine prophet.

God's spokesperson had to be an Israelite and not a foreigner (Num. 22:5ff.; Isa. 2:6). Just as Moses was the spokesperson for God, so every prophet after him would likewise speak for God (18:15). God had indeed called Moses to be Israel's leader, and at Mount Horeb, confronted by the awesome presence of the Lord, the people had also asked Moses to be their spokesperson (5:23–28). Future generations of prophets would also, like Moses, speak for God (18:16–18), and in fact, they testified that He put His words into their mouths (Jer. 1:9; 5:14; 20:8–9). The Israelites were under obligation to listen, but if they did not, they would have to give an account (18:19). When false prophets presumed to speak in the name of the Lord, the situation was similar to 13:1–5, but the genuine prophet did not have to use magic or cast spells; the true prophet already had a deep sense of commission to speak authoritatively in the name of the Lord (18:20).

The role of a genuine prophet was twofold: 1) to preach, challenging Israel to be loyal to her Lord; and 2) to utter predictions from the Lord. But how could the people test legitimate prophecy? The test of a true prophet was through verifying the short-range prophecies (fulfilled within a few days, a few months, or up to two years). As each of these short-period prophecies came true with one hundred percent accuracy, people were to realize they had a real prophet in their midst (see Jer. 28). Based on this test, believers could then be confident that these prophets could make predictions hundreds and even one or two thousand years in the future.

Later, in the Gospels, we see Jesus as a true prophet. His predictions of His death and resurrection came true. The traditional schooling in first-century Israel was that no Messiah was to die; rather, he was to appear and deliver Israel from her oppressors. Therefore, the disciples did not pay much attention to what Jesus said about the need for a Messiah to die. Peter, on one occasion, even took Jesus to task when He spoke of His death (Matt. 16:21–23). When the Messiah died on the cross, the disciples felt that their hope was lost, and they began to scatter. But Jesus' resurrection demonstrated the truth of His prophecies. The apostle John said that only after the resurrection did he believe all that Jesus had predicted (John 20:8). Once the disciples were convinced of Jesus' testimony as a legitimate prophet like Moses (Acts 3:23–24), they then confidently proclaimed Jesus' message of redemption and long-range prophecies.

**g. Crime and Punishment (19:1–21; 21:1–9, 22–23; 22:8); commandment 6 (5:17).** In the organization of the theocracy, one of the state's responsibilities for both civil and religious leaders was to make sure there would be no miscarriage of justice when dealing with matters of crime and punishment.[20]

**(1) Cities of Refuge (19:1–13).** Moses carefully prescribed the regulations for handling cases of murder and manslaughter. Before Moses' day, justice was carried out by family members who sought to avenge the blood of relatives who had been killed. To prevent any miscarriage of justice by overzealous people who could not distinguish properly between what was genuine murder or manslaughter, the state had to intervene and ensure proper justice for all concerned.

Moses describes the cities of refuge (Exod. 21:13–14), which were set aside in order to provide a haven for those involved in any offense affecting human life. After Israel would conquer the land (19:1), three cities were to be set aside on the west bank, in addition to three already set aside east of the Jordan River, making a total of six refuge towns (Num. 35:6–34; Josh. 20). The six cities were not named, but their central locations must have been accepted by the tribal leaders. Roads were to be prepared to provide easy access to these cities, enabling anyone who killed a man or woman to flee there (19:3).

If a person unintentionally killed a friend or neighbor (19:4)—for example, when chopping down a tree, the axehead flew off and struck the unfortunate victim (19:5–7)—the inno-

---

[20]Kaufman, "Structure of the Deuteronomic Law," p. 113.

cent offender was then to run immediately to a city of refuge to protect his or her own life. The state, represented by the elders of the city of refuge, took the responsibility to protect the innocent person (19:6–7). The elders could then assess the particulars of the case and declare that such a person was not worthy of death.

With the provision of the six cities of refuge for innocent people, Moses challenges Israel to be sensitive to the requirements of a holy and righteous God, and thereby also take care that no innocent blood be shed in the land. God's people were to take seriously their responsibilities to Him so that they would not be charged with the bloodshed of innocent people (19:8–10).

Moses then discusses the procedure for handling cases of deliberate murder (19:11–13). If a murderer fled into a city of refuge, the elders were to investigate. If they were convinced that the person had indeed committed premeditated murder, they were to turn the offender over to the dead person's relatives who would then execute the offender. The decisions by the elders of the cities of refuge were to be honorable and just. They must not permit themselves to be bribed lest God hold the nation accountable for the death of innocent people. Some people today feel that capital punishment is inhumane, but they must realize that God has committed to the state the responsibility of upholding justice in its courts, protecting the innocent victim, and making sure that the murderer pays for evil deeds. We are created in the image of God. But when anyone intentionally takes the life of another person, that very image is diminished, and for that reason, the murderer forfeits his or her life (Gen. 9:6). In later Judaism, precise laws were drawn up in order to insure justice in the court procedures, particularly in cases of murder (Mishnah, Sanhedrin). We need to recapture the righteous requirements of a holy God for our court systems today.

(2) The Test of Witnesses (19:15–21); commandment 9 (5:20). A basic guideline is that no single witness can testify against a person accused of any crime. Two or three witnesses are necessary before any charge can be investigated; the same truth applies within the body of Christ concerning an elder involved in wrongdoing (1 Tim. 5:19).

On certain occasions, one person (a malicious witness) might testify against what he or she considered to be a crime (literally, "a turning aside"), perhaps a defection from religious or civil prescriptions of the law (19:16). No local court could decide the particulars of this case. Both the accuser and the accused were sent to the central tribunal, "in the presence of the LORD" (19:17; 17:8–13). In such cases, the judges at the main tribunal would then have to make a thorough investigation, and once they determined that a witness had given false testimony, whereby an innocent person could have been killed for a crime he or she had not committed, the execution of justice was to be swift against the false witness (19:18–19). Such evil must be purged from the land, and the effect would be to discourage anyone else from being a false witness and to enable people to respect a holy God who detests liars.

The penalty for crimes came under the jurisdiction of the law of retaliation, *lex talionis* (Exod. 21:23–25; Lev. 24:17–21), the eye for an eye and tooth for a tooth. Some people feel such action is cruel, but this law provides for righteous judgment whereby the penalty fits the crime. In cases of premeditated murder, the crime of taking life from an innocent party is matched by the life taken from the offender. In judging the malicious liar, the punishment is based on the liar's intentions.

(3) **Anonymous Murder and its Atonement (21:1–9).** Moses provides guidelines for murders that have no known murderer. Rather than leave the case open, where perhaps one day the murderer might be found and brought to justice, it was necessary that atonement be made without delay for the crime. The law in this situation was particularly hard when the corpse of a murdered person was found in open country, apart from land worked by the farmers. Because a dead body pollutes the land which belongs to the Lord (Num. 35:34), steps had to be taken by the authorities to atone for it.

The elders and the judges of towns nearest the land on which the corpse was found would then have to measure the distance of the towns nearest to the body, and the leaders of the nearest town became responsible for it (21:2). They then took a heifer which had never been worked, led it down into a nearby valley which had not been plowed or planted, and where there

was a flowing stream; in that valley, the neck of the heifer was to
be broken. Unused land suggests that it had not been contami-
nated by human use, and therefore it could be used in atoning
for the dead person and the crime against the nation. Obviously,
the killing of the heifer in this procedure was not the normal
course provided for offering sacrifices when blood was shed
(21:3–4; Exod. 13:13).

What now follows is both a religious and judicial action.
The priests of the town responsible for the dead body were to
step forward and pronounce their blessings in accordance with
some liturgy, which was to settle any cases yet to be brought by
the victim's family regarding the deceased (21:5). In the judicial
action, the elders were to wash their hands over the heifer,
declaring their innocence of the crime (21:6–8). In their prayer,
they were to ask the Lord to accept this atonement on behalf of
*all* the people of Israel, indicating that the corpse had defiled
the entire land and not merely the town for which they were the
representatives. If they followed the procedure as directed by
God, then atonement was accepted and all guilt purged regarding the shedding of innocent blood. The leaders of the town
were to act responsibly in their relationship to the Lord in such
matters (21:9).

Note that there was no shedding of blood of the animal in
accordance with the Levitical procedure. But the animal was put
to death in place of the murdered and therefore the heifer
served as the substitute atonement. No avenger of blood was to
then hold anyone—much less the leaders of the town who tried
to care responsibly for the body of the dead person.

(4) **Corpses on Trees (21:22–23).** Pagan nations had a
horrid practice of placing the bodies of those condemned to
death either on poles or on walls, letting them hang indefinitely
for all to see (1 Sam. 31:10). By contrast, Israel was to treat
condemned people humanely. When prisoners or criminals
were put to death, their bodies were hung on trees or poles, but
they had to be taken down by sunset and buried. The injunction
to handle bodies in this manner was strict because such people
were cursed of God. If this instruction was disobeyed, then the
people and their land would become cursed (Lev. 18:24–27;
Num. 35:33–34). Paul also taught that inasmuch as the criminal

was cursed of God (Gal. 3:13), so Jesus likewise suffered and died as a criminal and was subjected to the gaze of the multitudes when He became the atonement for our sins.

(5) **Building Regulations (22:8).** When the Israelites built houses, they had to take care in building the roof, which had to have a parapet or wall around it for safety purposes. A lot of social life took place on the roofs in the Middle East during the summertime. People did household chores, entertained, and even slept on their roofs. If no parapet was present and a guest was injured or was killed by falling off the roof, the owner was liable for either manslaughter or criminal neglect. If the roof had a parapet and any accident did happen, the owner was not held responsible.

h. **War and the State (20:1–20; 21:10–14; 23:9–14; 25:17–19).** Although Moses had already given the people general guidelines for waging war (7:1–26), he now gives detailed instructions for battle strategy and other military information pertinent to the invasion and capture of the Promised Land.

(1) **Warning Not to Be Afraid (20:1–9).** Because the nations in the land were more numerous than Israel, with armies of horses and chariots (20:1), Israel might have the tendency to fear them. Moses charges Israel not to be afraid, because their God had already delivered them from Egypt and sustained them until a second generation reached the east bank of the Jordan River. God would also fight for Israel in their conquest of the Promised Land (20:1).

When Israel was about to go into battle, the priest was to address the troops and urge them not to fear any nation (20:2–4). God's people were not as well equipped as the pagan nations. Therefore, Israel needed to be encouraged and know that the Lord had all the battle strategies they would need to fight against the enemies. The troops were not to be fainthearted.

(2) **Army Exemptions (20:5–9).** Certain people were exempt from service in Israel's army. The officers established the categories of exemption from battle, which were humane considerations for young people facing combat for the first time. If some of them had not had opportunity to enjoy some of the ordinary affairs of life, they were to be separated from the

fighting troops (20:5–9). Those who were exempt from service included 1) the person who built a new house, but did not have it dedicated; 2) the person who planted a vineyard, but did not taste or enjoy it nor offer praise and prayer for it. (A five-year interval is indicated here: no fruit is used for the first three years of growth, the fourth year fruit is dedicated to the Lord, and only by the fifth year can any fruit be eaten [Lev. 19:23–25]); and 3) the person who recently became pledged to a woman but not yet married her. Israelite society wanted a man to be able to marry and have a family, rather than be killed in battle before he even had opportunity to have children to carry on his name.

We have already noted how Israel was humane in its treatment of servants, aliens, orphans, and widows, and now we see that military exemptions were also humane considerations that respected the value of human life. Some might accuse Israel of being only bloodthirsty and ready to kill without any humanitarian concerns, but these covenant provisions prove otherwise.

People were also exempted from military service if they proved to be fainthearted (20:8). To permit such soldiers to fight in the army would only be disastrous for their comrades-in-arms who would be psychologically affected in the battle. The wisest course would be to send these people home, not only for their own protection, but also to preserve the morale of the fighting troops.

Another humane consideration was for the recently married man (24:5). It would not be fair to separate a man from his wife in the early stages of their relationship, and he was granted exemption from military duty or any other responsibility. Every possibility was given for the couple to start a family. Any callous disregard in this matter could be criminal if the husband should suffer an untimely death, leaving a young bereaved widow with no children.

Finally, after the officers (or possibly tribal representatives) had arranged for the exemptions, army commanders were appointed to lead the troops into battle (20:9). Even though a lot of people were exempted, the remaining troops would be keen fighting men. Most important of all, the Lord Himself would go ahead of the army to insure victory.

(3) **Strategy in War (20:10–20).** Moses instructs the people in two war strategies against cities at a distance as well as cities in the land. The first instruction was for cities not in Canaan. When Israel would wage war against foreign nations, their cities were to be offered terms of peace, similar to those of the Middle Eastern treaties (20:10–15). If people surrendered peacefully and opened their gates to allow Israelite troops to enter, then the inhabitants became vassals of Israel and were placed under forced labor. But if the offer of peace was rejected, the Israelites were to put the city under siege, and when God gave them the victory, all of the foreign men, women, and children were put to death, and their livestock and possessions were plundered. However, if women were captured during military action, they were treated humanely (21:10–14). These instructions for Israel's warfare were far more considerate than the battle strategies of other nations.

The battle strategy for cities within the Promised Land was vastly different. After the Israelite armies would cross the Jordan River, they were to place all the inhabitants under the ban (*herem*) (20:16–18, 7:1–6; Josh. 6; 11:10–15; Judg. 7:25; etc.), which meant they were to be put to death. If Israel would not follow the Lord's command, the Canaanites would become a disastrous snare to His people. Our allegiance to the Lord can be no less, and even as Israel was called on to detest the practices of these nations, so the believer today should seriously consider the sins of our generation. Today we face the sins of abortion, homosexuality, lesbianism, drunkenness and so on, and while we are to exercise love and compassion for the sinner, we cannot condone the sinful practices.

Moses instructs the people that when they would lay siege against a city, they were not to touch the trees of the city (20:19–20). The usual practice was to cut down all of them so that they could be used for fuel and for building the siege works for cracking the city walls. Moses instructed Israel to exercise common sense and realize that fruit trees could provide food for the troops, while non-fruit trees were allowed to be cut down as needed. Once more, we see a humane consideration even for property, and in the long run, fruit trees could also provide food for conquered peoples and Israelites.

**(4) Women Prisoners of War (21:10–14).** When Israel captured a foreign nation and took women hostages, the Israelite soldiers were allowed to take the women as their wives. Under the humane consideration of the law, the female prisoner was to be taken home, her head shaved, her nails trimmed, and her clothes destroyed. These instructions were possibly for her purification as she was brought into a new experience. She was also given a month in which she could mourn her father (who probably was killed in the course of the military action) and her mother (who, if she remained alive, was serving another master). After the month had passed, the woman could then become the wife of her benefactor. These directives were humane in comparison with some of the practices of other nations in the Middle East who cruelly mistreated captured women.

An important question surfaces about the religion of this woman. Nothing is said in this passage, but the woman possibly adopted the faith of Israel and became a daughter of Israel. Another problem would be that of polygamy, because the soldier could have had another wife. At this period in Israel's history, polygamy was permitted to allow Israel to grow and also to make up for those who died in battle.

But the situation could arise in which the husband might feel the two were not compatible. He was permitted to divorce his wife ("let her go" is seen as divorce), but further stipulations protected her rights: her social status must not be changed (especially if she had converted to Israel's faith) and she was to be given some compensation. She could not be sold or treated as a slave (literally, "merchandise") and was free to go wherever she wanted.

**(5) Military Hygiene (23:9–14).** In any military action, men were brought together in close living quarters and good hygienic practice was necessary, not merely for its own sake, but for spiritual concerns as well. God was present in the camp to protect the army and also to deliver the enemies into their hands (23:14).

Therefore, the Israelite troops had to be very careful, keeping away from everything impure or unclean (from the Hebrew word *ra'*). The Hebrew word many times referred to what is morally impure, but here it could also mean what was an unpleasant and unclean situation (23:9).

One instance of uncleanliness was "nocturnal emission." This signified urine (or semen) involuntarily discharged or urine discharged in an unprescribed area because the person was too lazy to go to the areas designated for such purposes. The Israelite, in the morning, was to then go outside the camp and remain there until evening; he then had to bathe. Only after sundown could he reenter and rejoin his comrades. Not only would he have to endure separation from his friends but the officers would also be displeased. Everyone had to be hygenically clean and ritually pure (see also 23:12–14).

**i. Marriage Laws, Divorce, and Purity.** Kaufman sees this subject as an emphasis on commandment 7 (5:18).[21] But adultery is not the only consideration because other facets of these laws treat marriage, divorce and remarriage, and sexual purity.

**(1) Protecting the Newly Married Wife (22:13–21).** Should a husband, after his marriage had been consummated, declare that his wife had no tokens of virginity, the wife was protected by law. If she was found innocent, the husband had to pay a penalty. However, if the wife was not innocent, she was to be put to death for her indiscretion.

The Scripture does not say when the husband brought charges against his wife, but it must have been almost immediately after the wedding ceremonies. Verse 13 says that the husband thoroughly disliked his wife—he hated her, either for lack of compatibility or for suspicion that she had broken her engagement before the wedding, or whatever else. The specific charge was that he suspected that his wife was not a virgin at the consummation of the marriage (22:14).

The word "virginity" literally means "tokens of virginity." The commentaries suggest two possibilities: 1) the parents would want the evidence of the tokens which were the blood-stained sheets of the wedding night; or 2) if the wife was an adolescent, (from the Hebrew *betulim*) the evidence of regular menstruation after marriage could be obtained, unless she became pregnant immediately. The test of her integrity could also be determined by when the child was born; if it was born

---

[21] Ibid., pp. 113–14.

earlier than nine months after the wedding, then the husband had evidence that she indeed had been promiscuous.[22]

When a husband made such a charge, the girl's parents were to bring proof of her virginity—the blood-stained sheets or garments—to the town elders (22:15). Once a charge was made in public, the defense was also public, even though this might prove to be an embarrassing situation. The father was to explain to the elders that his son-in-law had brought slanderous charges against his daughter, and the only evidence needed to prove the charges wrong was either the blood-stained bedsheets of the wedding night or some other evidence of a blood-stained cloth of the woman's menstrual period (22:16–17). Once the elders had the evidence, they lost no time making a pronouncement of guilt and assigning charges (22:18–19): 1) the husband was to be punished; the Hebrew verb *misser* implies corporal punishment, possibly flogging; and 2) he was also fined one hundred shekels of silver, which were paid to the father as damages because the husband had dishonored his wife, her family, and Israel. Finally, no possibility for divorce was permitted, suggesting a very trying situation in the marriage relationship. The law prevented the husband from obtaining a divorce which was what he wanted in the first place.

If the husband's charge was true and no tokens of virginity or menstruation could be found, then the wife was to be executed by stoning, outside the door of her father's house. By marking the location of the execution, a stigma was now attached to the family, and it could be purged only by the father who had been dishonored. Even though the woman had not committed her indecency specifically in her father's house, her crime was charged to the family. While the father was not held responsible for his daughter's indiscretion, the father and the men of the town were to stone her to death to remove the disgrace from the dishonored family as well as from Israel. Is this a penalty beyond what can be assigned for the actual sin of fornication? Two reasons demonstrate that the penalty did fit the crime: 1) evil had been committed against Israel and against an Israelite family, and 2) no sacrifice was available in the Levitical

---

[22] Thompson, *Deuteronomy*, p. 236.

system to purge the sin of fornication or premeditated murder. The law also sought to make sure that if these sins were not curbed by drastic means, the danger was that they might spread among the people of God. These penalties for sin were to emphasize once more the holiness and righteousness of God and Israel's need to keep herself clean before Him.

(2) **Adultery and Rape (22:22–30).** A series of guidelines deal with a number of questionable relationships between a man and woman, based on commandment 7 (Lev. 18:20; 20:10). Other Middle Eastern documents had similar legislation. In the Hammurabi Code, the adulterous wife and her partner were drowned in water.[23]

(a) If a man was found sleeping with another man's wife, both people were to be put to death (22:22). Both had agreed to commit this sin and crime against not only the nation but also the Lord. Evil had to be purged out of Israel for the nation to remain sensitive to the holiness and righteousness of her God.

(b) If a man propositioned a woman who was already pledged to be married and they commit adultery, then both were to be taken outside of the gates of the city and stoned to death (22:23–24). The basis for the penalty is 1) she did not scream for help, which indicated her approval to the illicit sex act; 2) she was unfaithful to her soon-to-be husband; and 3) the man had violated another man's wife. If the young lady had screamed for help, the case would be considered rape.

(c) If in the countryside a man met a woman pledged to be married and he raped her, only the man was to be put to death. Because no one was around to hear the woman's screams for help, no wrongdoing can be charged to her (22:25–27). The law was humane and sought to protect the person's legitimate rights.

(d) If a man raped a virgin not pledged to be married and if the deed was discovered, he not only had to pay the young woman's father fifty shekels of silver (the price of a bride), but he also had to marry the woman. In raping her he established the union of husband and wife, and no divorce was possible (22:28–29). Furthermore, should the woman become pregnant as a result of the rape, the prohibition of divorce also protected the rights of the unborn child.

---

[23] Ibid., p. 237.

(e) No man may marry his father's wife, that is, have sex relationships with his stepmother (22:30; 27:20; Lev. 18:8; 20:11). Incestuous relationships were punished by the law in order to protect the sanctity of the family. The word "marry" literally means "to uncover his father's skirt," thereby violating his father's rights to his wife. While Middle Eastern people engaged in this practice, where perhaps a son may take over the wives of his deceased father, Israel's law prohibited this relationship.

The major thrust of these laws was to encourage monogamous marriages over that of polygamous ones, and even though it took a number of centuries to finally reach the goal, the ideal was in writing. In the modern world, the emphasis on purity and sanctity is what is necessary to protect the institution of the family. Believers should take every effort to ensure that the family remains intact, and young people should be taught very carefully what is acceptable and undesirable in sexual matters.

(3) **Marriage, Divorce, and Remarriage (24:1–4).** Divorce is not specifically considered, but instructions carefully prescribe remarriage.

The reason for divorce is that a husband became displeased with his wife because he found something indecent about her (literally, "nakedness of a thing"). The meaning of this is not given. Certainly it could not mean adultery; there was no call for her death (22:22).

In sending away his wife, the husband only had to write her a certificate of divorce, a document of "cutting off," which he gave to her when she left. It is questionable whether true believers (the remnant) would have been involved in such a practice. But we must remember that many Israelites were not true believers. The purpose of the law, then, was to be a schoolmaster to bring unbelievers to a knowledge of salvation and to a genuine belief in Israel's God. But until an unbelieving husband came to faith in the Lord, he could divorce his wife.

Once the wife was sent away, she could remarry (24:2). But what would happen to her if her second husband also gave her a certificate of divorce because he hated her or if her marriage bond was dissolved when he died (24:3)? The law specifically declared that this woman must not return to her first husband to be married to him again because such a union was defiling (24:4).

What is the point of these laws? According to some, remarriage to a first husband was considered adultery, because from his point of view she had already been married to another man. Another view is that such a union would be highly distasteful. Whatever the reason, the law served as a deterrent for such situations and encouraged the wife's marriage to her second husband to remain intact. At least the second husband must realize that his wife was not permitted to return to her first husband. The law was not able to solve all of the problems of divorce and remarriage, but at least some of the excesses of allowing women to be passed from one man to another would be minimized.

Jesus taught that from the beginning marriage was considered a lifelong commitment (Matt. 19:3–6; Gen. 2:24). Within the body of Christ today, the ideal is that almost all cases of divorce would be forbidden. The only question is the exception clause for divorce when there was marital unfaithfulness (Matt. 19:8–9).

**(4) Transvestites and Paganism (22:5).** Women were prohibited from wearing not only men's clothing but also all that pertains to a man—his weapons, ornaments, and so on. Neither were men to wear anything pertaining to women. The prohibitions could refer to deviant sexual behavior or transvestism when the male-female orders are reversed. Homosexual behavior is detestable to the Lord (Lev. 18:22; 20:13), and the legislation insists that there must be a difference between the roles of man and woman. In the ancient world, the pagans practiced deviant sexual behavior for cultic purposes, but Israel was to studiously avoid such unacceptable behavior.

**(5) Mutilation (23:1).** God instructed His covenant people to appear before Him during the three major pilgrimage festivals (Exod. 23:14–17), but He also specified who was permitted to enter into the assembly for worship in the convocation. Guidelines were provided to insure purity of the worshipers in the sacred sanctuary.

Men who were mutilated in their sexual organs were barred from worship in the assembly of God's people. The reasons were both religious (Lev. 21:6, 8) and physical (Lev. 21:20; 22:24). Sacred worship required not only a proper heart attitude but also a regard for one's own body. Because the Canaanites imposed castration on certain people in their sanctuary worship, Moses forbade any such practices among the Israelites.[24] Once again we note that there must be a sharp distinction between the worship systems. When a person was castrated against his will, however, he could still experience the blessings of the Lord; in such circumstances he was not responsible (Isa. 56:3–5).

(6) **The Bastard (23:2; Hebrew 23:3).** The Hebrew term for bastard, *mamzer,* is used only here and in Zechariah 9:6 in the Old Testament Scriptures. The meaning of the term is difficult to ascertain. Later Jewish commentators define it as children born of incest, although others apply the word to offspring of Israelites and non-Israelites, Philistines (Zech. 9:6), Ammonites or Moabites (Neh. 13:23). In either case, the children of these dubious unions were barred from the congregation in worship, even to the tenth generation. This guideline also sought to ensure the purity of family relationships and the marriage tie between husband and wife within Israel.

(7) **Cult Prostitutes (23:17–18).** The law condemned illicit sexual behavior in general, but to become involved as a prostitute in the pagan shrines was particularly singled out for censure. Violations of this prohibition became rampant across the centuries, by both men and women who became cult prostitutes in Israel. The prophets denounced this practice with the utmost severity (1 Kings 15:12; 2 Kings 23:7). In one specific instance, Hosea's wife became involved in this practice, and he sought to win her back, time and time again (Hos. 3:1–2).

No money earned from being a prostitute was ever to be used for any vow in the house of the Lord. The male prostitute was called a "dog" (Hebrew) as a way of expressing total revulsion of using such wages in the worship of Israel's God.

(8) **Levirate Marriages (25:5–10).** The term "levirate" comes from Latin *levir,* meaning brother-in-law or the husband's brother. This ancient practice was used in the ancient laws of the Middle East as well as in Israel (Gen. 38). Moses specified

---

[24] Ibid., p. 239.

that when a husband died without leaving an heir, his widow must remain within the family. The dead man's brother was to marry her and "perform the duty of a husband's brother to her" (25:5 NASV). The first child born of this union became the heir of the deceased so that his name could be maintained in Israel. If no children were born to carry on the line of a husband, then his name was blotted out from the community of God's people. Levirate marriages were a means to evade such a dreadful possibility.

Opportunity was given to the brother-in-law to refuse his obligations, but the law made it quite difficult to do so because of the pressure on him. When he decided not to marry the widow, she then pled her case before the elders at the town gate. If the brother-in-law publicly persisted in his refusal before the leaders, the widow then took off one of his sandals, implying that he did not wish to accept his responsibility, and also spat in his face to humiliate and shame him. Ever afterward, the house of the brother-in-law carried the stigma, "the house of him whose sandal is removed" (25:10 NASV).

In many cases, however, the brother-in-law could have had legal reasons for not wishing to marry the widow. Such was the case in Ruth 4:7–8, where the nearest of kin to Boaz felt that there could have been a legal snag in property claims between his own estate and that of Ruth's former husband if a son were born to continue the line of the deceased husband. Boaz was the next of kin and was quite able and willing to marry Ruth to raise up children to her former husband, but the nearest of kin did take off his sandal in public, thereby publicly refusing to accept his responsibility. It would appear in this case there was no further stigma on his name.

**j. Stealing and Violation of Property.** These laws most closely relate to commandment 8 (5:19).[25] The law valued a person's integrity not to take what belonged to either God or other people.

**(1) A Neighbor's Property (22:1–4).** Israelites were not to ignore or have designs on stray animals; they were to return them to the owner (22:1). Even if the Israelite lived at a great

---

[25] Kaufman, "Structure of the Deuteronomic Law," p. 114.

distance from the owner or did not know to whom the animals belonged, the Israelite was to hold the animals in trust until the neighbor came looking for them (22:2). Lost clothing was to be returned as well (22:3). Israel was a household, and every person was to look out for the other person's interests. One's obligation also extended to helping animals to their feet if they had fallen down; the law even had a humane interest in the care for beasts of burden. Moses upheld the law that required an Israelite to help even enemies with stray animals (Exod. 23:4–5). Deuteronomy makes only quick reference to the care of animals, but the instructions in Exodus were to also be observed. The lesson is plain; a person's neighbor is everyone in need, a lesson that Jesus drew on in Luke 10:30–37.

(2) **Charging Interest (23:19–20).** In Moses' day, financial arrangements were simple, and loans were easily made in times of crisis (Exod. 22:25; Lev. 25:35–37). Many Middle Eastern countries charged exorbitant interest rate for such loans.[26] In contrast to this practice, an Israelite was never to charge interest from his brother Israelite when the latter was in dire straits, for two reasons: 1) Israel was a covenant community where each Israelite—poor, middle class, or rich—was equal before the Lord; and 2) the poor Israelite should not be humiliated by having to pay interest. If God could bountifully provide for Israel with every good thing, then how could the wealthy person, benefiting from God's liberality, turn around and mistreat a fellow Israelite? Charging interest was stealing, and the rich only made themselves obnoxious by trying to make a profit on a person's misery.

An Israelite could charge interest on loans made to a foreigner who was possibly a traveling merchant and not a part of the covenant community. Any money loaned to him was considered strictly a business deal.

(3) **Take Care When Making Vows (23:21–23).** Israelites were allowed to make vows to the Lord, but once a vow was made, they must not only do what was promised, but also perform it as soon as possible. Not keeping the vow was a sin; it robbed God of what had been promised. It was better not to vow than to be a liar (12:6–11, 17, 26).

---

[26]Thompson, *Deuteronomy*, p. 242.

(4) **Have Concern for a Neighbor's Crops (23:24–25).** When people traveled from one part of the country to another, they were permitted to satisfy their immediate thirst and hunger by picking what grapes and kernels of grain they needed. The owner of the field was merely being hospitable and generous to the travelers. But such privileges were not to be exploited by putting grapes into one's basket or cutting down standing grain and carrying it off. Owners, too, had property rights, and travelers must remember that they are guests of a generous host. To remove property was the same as stealing.

(5) **Laws About Kidnapping (24:7).** The worst case of stealing was to kidnap someone and sell the person into slavery, thereby earning a profit (5:19; Exod. 21:16). The practice was quite common in the Middle East, and many of the law codes had legislation curbing the stealing of a life. Kidnapping for profit in Israel was also called murder because even though the victim did not actually die, he or she was cut off from the covenant people. The kidnapper, therefore, was put to death in order to purge evil from the community of God. The judgment was equitable because if the victim was to be cut off from his or her people, the life of the kidnapper must also be cut off.

(6) **Compassion for the Poor Servant (24:14–15).** Another serious form of stealing was to withhold the wages of the poor and needy. The words "do not take advantage" are literally "you shall not oppress." This law applied to both Israelites and alien residents. The wealthy were charged not to hire extra help among those less fortunate and then steal their wages. Poor people needed the money at the end of the day to buy food or whatever else their families needed. This humane law called for fair treatment for those less fortunate.

When poor people were oppressed by wealthy employers, the poor were told to ask God for help; He will listen and hold the offenders guilty for their sin. Great will be the judgment on the rich who cause such hardship within the household of Israel. Those who were wealthy were told to always remember that their forebears once had been poor and needy slaves in Egypt. James referred to this very passage when directing the rich to be responsible and help the poor; if they would not listen, God had His way to judge the offenders (James 5:1–6).

(7) **Correct Weights and Measures (25:13–16).** The laws demanded honest dealings in business; no stealing was permitted at the expense of the buyer. The seller was not to have "an undue thumb on the scales" to fatten his own account. Such disregard of decency could only invite God's severe condemnation.

The laws prohibited the use of two kinds of weights or volume measures. Using only one set of weights and measures ensured the purchasers that they were getting exactly what they were paying for (Lev. 19:35–36). Amos denounced such people in his generation for not having any integrity (Amos 8:5). God detests and will condemn those who are dishonest and unrighteous in business dealings. Dishonesty will only shorten lives.

(8) **Moving the Neighbor's Boundary Lines (19:14).** The land was yet to be conquered by the second generation and succeeding generations, but Israel must remember that the landowner was the Lord. As the tribal lines were marked off by Joshua (chap. 13–19), each family had to realize that they shared in the Lord's inheritance as long as they lived on His land. When a greedy person or rich landowner tried to steal from his neighbor by moving boundary stones, they were stealing from God (Prov. 23:10; Isa. 5:8; Hos. 5:10). God's only recourse was to judge the offender and curb the greediness in Israel.

**k. Miscellaneous Religious and Civil Law Codes.** The rest of Moses' message (to 25:19) is what Kaufman calls "extraneous material" because it is difficult to classify.

(1) **The First-born Have Rights (21:15–17).** The law sought to curb the possibility of favoritism in a polygamous home where children of a beloved wife might have more privileges than children of a less-loved wife. Jacob, for example, loved Rachel more than Leah (Gen. 29:30–31). Therefore, when the father settled the inheritance rights for his family, he was not allowed to let his emotions overrule fair play. The usual practice was that the first-born took precedence over all of the other sons, but there are many occasions in Scripture where the law of primogeniture was changed so that the younger displaced the elder: Isaac and Ishmael, Jacob and Esau, Ephraim and Manasseh, and Solomon and his older brothers, for example. These were special circumstances guided by God, but the family

obviously suffered tensions as a result. One must also consider that the first-born belonged to God, and his rights were not to be degraded, even if he was the son of the hated wife. Furthermore, if the first-born was the son of the less-loved wife, he was to receive double (literally, "mouth of two"), which marked him the favored one.

(2) **Rebellious Sons (21:18–21).** When parents had a son who was stubborn and rebellious in spite of discipline, their authority was in danger. Parents had to be firm in their relationships with their children, and the community lent their support to the father in these circumstances. A rebellious son dishonored not only his parents but also God.

The parents were to take their rebellious son to the town elders who had the task of preserving both the social order and the sanctity of the family (21:19). The parents were instructed to tell the elders that their son was disobedient, stubborn, rebellious, a profligate (a glutton), and a drunkard (21:20). The actual crime was not the lifestyle chosen by the son but his disobedience to his parents' authority. The case became a community responsibility.

When all of the evidence had been turned over and examined by the elders, judgment was passed on behalf of the entire nation, and the son was stoned to death if he was found guilty. The fifth commandment has been designated as a commandment of promise, and children who honor their parents are promised long life. The law implies, then, that if children are disobedient, their lives are in danger of being shortened. This truth, also carried over into the New Testament (Eph. 6:1–4), is still true today. Many believing parents confess that despite good discipline, their son or daughter has gone astray, cutting short his or her own life.

(3) **Saving the Mother Bird (22:6–7).** Another humane directive peculiar to Deuteronomy was that while young birds might be taken either for food or pets, the mother bird was to be released. The normal choice would be to take both mother bird and the young for food, but by releasing the mother bird, the possibility of a future supply of food was assured. Israelites were discouraged from large-scale killing of foul, reflecting some of the modern conservation concerns.

**(4) Unnatural Mixing and Sanctification (22:9–11).** Unnatural mixing was already forbidden (22:5; Lev. 19:19), suggesting primarily theological concerns that sought to maintain distinctions in the created order.[27] The injunction applied to mixing seeds in the vineyard, using two kinds of animals for plowing, and mixing various kinds of fibers when weaving cloth. If a farmer planted rows of grain between rows of vines in a vineyard and also mixed vines and fruit trees together in the same area, the injunction was that both grain and fruit must be forfeited (literally, "consecrated") to the sanctuary. Perhaps the directive was against the standard Egyptian practice, and God wanted a difference between what the Egyptians did and what the Israelites were to do.

**(5) Tassels for Acceptable Garments (22:12).** Tassels were to be attached to the four corners of one's garment as a reminder to Israel to be obedient to the commandments (Num. 15:37–41). Men were challenged to let even their clothing mark them as a people set apart by God to serve Him in the covenant relationship.

**(6) Who May Enter the Assembly of the Lord (23:1–8; Hebrew 23:2–9).** Since Israel belonged to the Lord, the identity of who worshiped with God's people was important. We already know that persons born of an illegitimate marriage and emasculated persons were not allowed to enter the sanctuary (23:1–2). But Moses also specifically barred the Ammonites and Moabites from the assembly, even to the tenth generation (23:3–7). Remember that the Ammonites failed to offer bread and water to Israel when they had come out of Egypt, and the Moabites had actually hired Balaam to curse Israel so that God in turn would break His promises to them (Num. 22–24). God, however, changed Balaam's message to blessing because no person can curse Israel contrary to His word given to the nation. As a result, Israel was not to enter into any negotiated pacts of peace and friendship with these peoples.

Two other peoples were to be treated more leniently: the Edomites and the Egyptians (23:7–8). Israel once lived in Egypt as aliens, and the Edomites were related to the Israelites

---

[27]Keil and Delitzsch, *Pentateuch*, p. 410.

because Esau and Jacob were brothers. If Edomites or Egyptians desired to live in Israel as aliens, then the third generation of their children could enter into the congregation of Israel as full members. Unfortunately, the leniency shown to Edom did not last; when Judah was defeated by Babylon, Edom so gloated over Judah's downfall that both Obadiah and Ezekiel condemned the Edomites (Obad; Ezek. 35; 36:1–7).

(7) **Runaway Slaves (23:15–16; Hebrew 23:16–17).** The passage seems to describe a runaway slave from a foreign country. Care for Hebrew slaves already has been mentioned (15:12–18), but the law was also humane, directing that foreign runaways were not to be returned to their former master. Runaway slaves were permitted to live wherever they wanted in Israel, and they were protected from greedy people who might want to enslave them for life since they had no rights. The laws of other Middle Eastern countries prescribed death to runaway slaves who were apprehended.[28] In contrast, Israel was to remember they, too, had once been slaves, and therefore the foreigner in their midst was not to be mistreated.

(8) **No Pledging of Millstones (24:6).** The lender was not to take interest from a poor and needy Israelite (23:19–20), but the borrower had to provide some kind of collateral as a sign that he would eventually make good on his loan. If he didn't repay the loan, the collateral was to be forfeited. But the law stated that the lender could not take as collateral a pair of millstones, not even only the upper one. Two millstones were used to grind grain; the bottom one remained stationary while the upper one revolved, crushing the grain. Wives used the mill to grind enough grain for the daily bread, but to take the mill or even a part of it would take the borrower's very life. Only enough collateral was needed to ensure the repayment of a loan.

(9) **Caring for Leprosy (24:8–9).** Leprosy (*ṣara'at*) here is not today's Hansen's disease which first affects the skin, nerves, and muscles in the arms and legs, eventually crippling a person. The Scripture refers to a variety of infectious diseases (Lev. 13–14), rot, and fungi affecting clothing and houses (Lev. 14:55). The priests were not only to treat these diseases very

---

[28]Thompson, *Deuteronomy*, p. 241.

carefully, following the Levitical instructions to curb its spread, but also to minister to the healed person during the period of restoration into the community.

**(10) Concern About Loans (24:10–13).** In addition to the laws about collateral (24:6), Moses also provides further directives to protect the poor and needy. While security was necessary for the loan, the lender must not enter the house of the borrower and grab what he would consider as collateral. The lender was to remain outside and permit the recipient of the loan to provide a suitable article to guarantee the loan. The law was designed to let the borrower retain some dignity in proving assurance that the loan would be repaid. The very poor person's only collateral might be his own cloak. If the cloak was used as collateral, it was taken only during the daytime hours; by sunset the cloak was to be returned so that the poor man would have a garment to cover himself during the night.

**(11) Each One Responsible for His Own Sin (24:16).** This one-sentence legislation is extremely important because the law called for individual responsibility for one's own deeds. If a son was condemned to death for his evil deeds, the father was not to be put to death also; neither was the son to die for his father's wickedness. And yet, a parent's wrongdoing can affect the children and grandchildren (5:9), who may repeat their parent's sins. The law is fair in that each person pays for his or her own sins.

**(12) Regard for the Alien, Orphan, and Widow (24:17–22).** Additional directives are given for the care of the poor and needy (see also 14:29). Farmers were challenged to leave any sheaves of grain overlooked in the harvest. When olive tree branches were beaten for olives, the farmer was to take only those which fell after the first beating; he was not to pick the olives left on the trees. Only the first picking of grapes was to be gathered; what grew afterward was to be left on the vine. The poor and needy could go into the fields, vineyards, and orchards and gather whatever was available at the time. This food was God's gift for the poor through the generosity of the farmers. (We read of this kind of gleaning in Ruth 2, when Ruth gleaned in Boaz' field.) Finally, the farmers were reminded that their forebears were once slaves in Egypt, dependent on what the

Egyptian master would provide. In the name of the Lord, therefore, provision was to be made for the poor and needy.

**(13) Legal Disputes, but Limits to Punishment (25:1–3).** Laws also determined when and how much corporal punishment was to be given (see 22:18). The guilty person was to be given a punishment proportionate to the violation, but must not pay more than the crime deserved. In a legal dispute, the case would be taken to court, where judges would render a decision either to acquit (justify) the innocent or condemn the offender.

If a judge found an offender guilty, he set the penalty and the offender was flogged in his presence. The judge carefully determined the number of lashes to be given to the offender, but never was the penalty to be more than forty lashes. In this way, the offender would not be humiliated and reduced to the level of an animal. Other Middle Eastern nations had similar systems of justice, and these systems also set forty lashes as the maximum for corporal punishment.[29] Later Judaism sought to be somewhat lenient with the maximum punishment; no one was to be flogged for more than thirty-nine lashes (*Makkot,* III, 13, 14).[30] Paul received this type of punishment five times (2 Cor. 11:24).

**(14) Do Not Muzzle the Ox (25:4).** In the ancient world, grain was threshed on a high hill, where an ox (or horse) pulled a threshing-sledge across piles of grain. The heavy sledge, with sharp poles on the bottom on which stones were attached, separated the grain and chaff. On a windy day, grain and chaff were thrown into the air, and the chaff was blown away while the grain fell back onto the ground (Ps. 1:4). When the ox was hungry, he could eat some of the grain (Prov. 12:10).

Paul used this verse to establish that "the laborer is worthy of his hire" (1 Cor. 9:9; 1 Tim. 5:18). If a faithful ox was allowed to eat some of the master's grain, then the servants of God should also share in a portion of the blessings the Lord would provide for His people. No one should withhold care from the faithful servant who labors for the benefit of God's people.

---

[29] Ibid., p. 250.

[30] Herbert Danby, *The Mishnah, Makkot* 3:10–15 (London: Oxford University Press, 1933), pp. 407–8.

(15) **Interfering in a Brawl (25:11–12).** The law also regulated the penalties involving fights between Israelites, particularly if the wife of one of the contenders seized the private parts of her husband's assailant. No other such legislation is mentioned in the Pentateuch, although there are other instructions dealing with men involved in fighting (Exod. 21:12–15, 18–26). One could not fault the wife for aiding her husband, but the way she sought to help was considered odious, and therefore her hand was to be cut off. One reason for this severe penalty was the possibility that she could have caused permanent injury to her husband's opponent and prevented him from having any children. The penalty was the application of the *lex talionis*—eye for an eye, tooth for a tooth—(19:21), because if the woman caused her husband's assailant such harm that he would be rendered childless, then the loss of her hand would match the crime.

(16) **Remember What Amalek Did (25:17–19).** The Ammonites are again mentioned because not only were they barred from the assembly of the Lord (23:3–6), but Israel was warned to have nothing whatsoever to do with them. They were to be blotted out of Israel's memory forever. Some reasons for such treatment were: 1) the stragglers of Israel were cut down while in the wilderness (Exod. 17:8–16); 2) the Amalekites, along with the Canaanites, cut down many in Israel after the Kadesh-Barnea affair (Num. 14:39–45); and 3) Israel suffered much from Amalek (1 Sam. 14:48; 27:8–9; 30:1–20; 2 Sam. 8:12), across the years. By the time of Hezekiah, these offensive people had ceased to be an organized nation (1 Chron. 4:43).

### 3. Responsibility for Firstfruits and Tithes (26:1–15)

In the last part of his second address, Moses instructs the people about firstfruits and the third-year tithes for the poor and needy (see 18:4; Exod. 23:19; Num. 18:12ff.; etc.).

**a. The Firstfruits Belong to the Lord (26:1–11).** When Israel would settle down in the land and begin to enjoy God's blessings, they were to take the firstfruits of all they had produced, place them in an approved basket, and proceed to the shrine of God's approval (26:1–2). As each Israelite man presented his basket to the priest in office at the time (the chief

priest at the sanctuary, 1 Sam. 1:9; 2:13–16), he was to declare
that he had come to the land promised by the Lord God of Israel
(26:3). Each generation, as they made this pronouncement,
would affirm that they are one with the generation which
entered the Promised Land under Joshua, proclaiming thereby a
continual thanksgiving for God's faithfulness. The priest then
placed the basket in front of the altar of the Lord (26:4).

Gerhard von Rad suggests that 26:5–10 forms a creed which
was recited when the firstfruits were offered. Since there is no
mention of Mount Sinai or Mount Horeb in it, he feels it was
added later.[31] Derek Kidner questions whether such a creed
existed at the time of early Israel.[32] It would seem the Shema
(6:4–9) would be more of a creedal statement than this passage.

The Israelites brought their firstfruits as a visible expression
of their gratitude to God. As they brought the basket to the
priests at the designated place, they would stand before the altar
and recount how God had delivered them from their slavery and
was faithful to bring them into the Promised Land to enjoy His
blessings.

The phrases "wandering Aramean" (26:5) or "a Syrian ready
to perish" (26:5 KJV) seem to refer to Jacob. The Hebrew word
'oved, rendered "wandering" or "ready to perish," usually
means "perish" or "die," but at times it can also mean "lost"
(22:3). The Hebrew term suggests that Jacob, as a wanderer,
faced danger many times. Aram is the area to which Jacob fled
after tricking Isaac (Gen. 29), and Rachel and Leah originated
there. From Jacob came twelve sons and eventually the entire
family of seventy people (Exod. 1:5) who went to Egypt. From
this small family came a nation favored of the Lord. But when
the Israelites were enslaved, their misery and pressure were so
great that they cried to God who heard and delivered them
"with a mighty hand and outstretched arm" (26:8). The God of
Israel was the one true God, who accomplished His purposes for
His people and would bring them to the Promised Land flowing
with milk and honey (see 6:1–3). The Israelites would climax
their statement by saying, "And now I bring the firstfruits of the

---

[31] von Rad, *Deuteronomy*, pp. 151ff.
[32] Derek Kidner, "The Origins of Israel," *The Student Fellowship Bulletin* 57
(1970), pp. 3–12, (InterVarsity Christian Fellowship publication).

soil that you, O LORD, have given me" (26:10). They would place the basket before the Lord and bow (prostrate themselves) in worship. They were then to rejoice with the Levites and aliens in the good things the Lord could provide (26:11). Each generation was to give thanks to God and bless His name for His great and mighty deeds.

**b. Carefully Handling the Tithes for the Poor (26:12–15).** In the third year, the year of the tithe (26:12), the Israelites were to gather a tithe to give to the poor. Because these tithes were not directly controlled by the priests, Moses gave instructions to avoid their misuse. The Israelites had to make a statement before the Lord that the tithes were used as He had specified (26:13–14). The most likely time for the declaration would have been during the Feast of Tabernacles, after the general harvest, when this particular tithe was out of his hand, "removed from my house" (26:13).

The Israelites testified in negatives: 1) they had not eaten any of the sacred portion while in mourning; 2) they had not cared for their own personal tithe while in an unclean state (at which time they were not even permitted to be in the community); and 3) they had not offered any of this tithe to the dead (14:1). The last one in particular may have been a Canaanite ritual, and no one was to be involved in these practices at all.[33]

The Israelites were instructed to end their statement with a prayer to God to look down from heaven—His residence—and abundantly bless Israel and the land as He Himself had promised to the forefathers (26:15).

### 4. Ratifying the Covenant (26:16–19)

With this short passage, Moses concludes the code (although the second message continues to 28:68). What was stated in 12:1 is now seen again in 26:16; the agreement is to be ratified, with Moses acting as the mediator between the Lord and Israel. The leadership was to declare on behalf of the Israelites that the Lord was their God and that they would walk in His ways; keep His decrees, commands, and laws; and obey

---

[33] Thompson, *Deuteronomy*, pp. 257–58.

Him. In a sense Israel made a formal commitment to the treaty or covenant drawn up between God and His people.

In turn the Lord also gives His word, declaring that the Israelites are His people. God will give them praise, fame, and honor if they will obey Him.

## B. The Commandment to Renew the Covenant (27:1–26).

The details of the law-code (Deut. 12–26) are placed in Deuteronomy *after* the first mention of renewing the covenant (11:26–32) and *before* the second mention of renewing the covenant (27:1–26). Some commentators have considered it strange that the anticipation of renewing the covenant in the future in the Promised Land should come before its actual ratification on the east bank of the Jordan River in chapter 28.[34] But it is not necessary to look for strict chronological patterns, and it would be natural for Moses to anticipate its ratification in the Promised Land even before he outlined the details of the code. Moses also sought to encourage his people to think of giving their hearts in service to the Lord their God by being obedient to the covenant.

### 1. Preparations for Renewal (27:1–8)

It appears that the joint responsibility of Moses and the elders was to impress upon the latter that once they were in the land, the covenant would have to be ratified. After Israel would cross the Jordan River into the land, large stones were to be coated with plaster, and the law was to be written (engraved) on them (27:2–4, 8). Such practices probably took place in Egypt, except that the Egyptians painted their text inscriptions on stones or walls. The stones would be a witness to future generations of the covenant between God and His people. The phrase "all the words of this law" (27:8) is couched in general terms, referring to either chapters 12 to 26 or only the covenant given at Mount Horeb.

After the second generation would cross the Jordan River and arrive at Mount Ebal and Mount Gerizim, they were to ratify the covenant (Josh. 8:30–35). An important trade route

---

[34] Ibid., pp. 260–262.

passed between the mountains, and on the east end of the pass was the important town of Shechem, where both Abraham and Jacob had built altars (Gen. 12:6–7; 33:18–20). Furthermore, Joseph's bones were to be buried in this general area as well (Josh. 24:32). Here at Mount Ebal, Israel was to set up her altar in the prescribed manner (Exod. 20:25), using no iron tool (27:5–6). The inscribed stones were set in place adjacent to the altar, and in this strategic place the covenant was to be renewed within the Promised Land. Even though a central sanctuary would be located in Shiloh later on in Samuel's day, there was no doubt that the Lord could choose any place He designated where His name should be located, including Shechem, until the time when there would be a central sanctuary only in Jerusalem.

Burnt offerings and peace offerings were to be presented; the former emphasized dedication while the latter were to be eaten in a fellowship meal (27:6–7; Exod. 24:5). One final note emphasizes the manner in which the words of the law were to be engraved on the stones (27:8). Each word must be clear and easily read. Ideally, these words would also be engraved on the people's hearts and minds, ever reminding them to be obedient to God.

## 2. Israel Challenged About the Covenant (27:9–10)

Once again, both Moses and the priests challenged the Israelites to be silent and listen to God's directives so that they would obey Him and follow His commands and decrees (see also 26:16–19).

## 3. The Blessings and the Curses (27:11–26)

After giving instructions about the future ratification of the covenant, Moses describes the ceremony of the blessings and the curses.

a. The Blessings (27:11–12). The six tribes who were descendants of Leah and Rachel (Simeon, Levi, Judah, Issachar, Joseph, and Benjamin) were to stand on the slopes of Mount Gerizim. Their task was to bless the people. The ark, which housed the covenant tablets, was located between Mount Gerizim and Mount Ebal. On the slopes of Mount Ebal stood

Reuben and Zebulun (sons of Leah) and Dan, Naphtali, Gad, and Asher (sons of the maidservants). The picture was symbolic: there was no possibility for any in-between conduct. The Israelites could choose either to obey the covenant and enjoy God's blessings or to do evil and suffer God's curses.

What is puzzling is the absence of any mention of blessings; we are not sure why they are omitted. In the interpretation provided by the *Mishnah*, Tractate *Sota* 7:4, the Levites, standing by the ark, were to address the blessings to Mount Gerizim, and the six tribes standing there were to respond with the "Amen."[35] Then the Levites in turn were to address the curses to the tribes on Mount Ebal, and the tribes standing there were also to respond with the "Amen." The blessings could be implied to be the exact opposite of the curses mentioned here, even as in 28:3–6 and 16–19, where the direct opposites are set out in order.

**b. The Curses (27:13–26).** A list of twelve curses, sometimes designated as the Dodecalog, are proclaimed. As each curse is pronounced, all the people were to respond with a resounding, "Amen" (see also Num. 5:22; 1 Kings 1:36; Neh. 5:13; 8:6; etc.). As the people approved of each curse, they were declaring that any time they or their descendants—as each of them would also have to assent in future renewals of the covenant—failed to be responsible before God, the consequences would be drastic.

The first curse condemns the person who would carve an image or cast an idol (27:15). The longest description of all curses, and first on the list, is the condemnation of a person who yields allegiance to a foreign god. Such wickedness is nothing less than a breakdown of commandments 1 and 2. What makes the crime worse is that pagan worship is practiced in secret as if God cannot see what goes on in the dark. Tragically, future generations did become involved in such detestable practices (Isa. 44:9–20; Jer. 10:1–16).

The second curse is a judgment against one who would dishonor or despise his or her father and mother, which is a breakdown of commandment 5 (27:16; 21:18–21). While the

---

[35] Danby, *The Mishnah,*

prosecution of a stubborn son or daughter involves an emotional strain on the family, this curse was intended as a deterrent to wayward behavior of sons and daughters.

The third curse relates to property rights (19:14) and moving boundary stones (which was considered stealing), which is against commandment 8 (27:17). The fourth curse was pronounced against the person who would lead astray the blind (27:18), because the less fortunate of society are under God's special care (Lev. 19:14). The scope of this curse has a wider meaning, however, because it is a warning against anyone who would take advantage of any unfortunate person. A fifth curse gave the alien, orphan, and widow protection against injustice (27:19; 24:17).

The next four curses attempt to prevent a breakdown of commandment 7 within the society. Illicit sex is detestable to God (Lev. 18:6–23), and the possibilities are: the person who sleeps with his father's wife (the stepmother, 27:20; 22:30; Lev. 18:8; 20:11); the one who commits bestiality (27:21; Exod. 22:19; Lev. 18:23; 20:15); the man who has sex relations with his sister (27:22), and the rule also applies to a brother and sister who have only one parent in common; and finally, the person who has relations with his mother-in-law (27:23; Lev. 18:17; 20:14).

The tenth and eleventh curses relate to murder, addressed in commandment 6. The tenth curse condemns the killer who secretly plots to kill another person (27:24; Exod. 21:12; Ps. 10:8) and whose identity is unknown. Even though the killer can never be brought to trial, God has already pronounced judgment. The eleventh curse condemns the assassin who seeks gain from the crime (27:25; 16:19; Lev. 19:15, 35).

The twelfth and last curse is all-inclusive; the person who does not keep all of the law (*Torah*) is cursed. The first eleven curses are examples, but the twelfth curse will be applied to a person who does not abide by the words of the law.

## C. The Covenant Directives on the East Bank of the Jordan (28:1–68; Hebrew 28:1–69).

Here Moses describes the actual renewal of the covenant by the second generation on the east bank. When comparing the blessings and curses, it might appear strange that more curses are mentioned than blessings. This phenomena also appears in the Middle Eastern treaties.[36] From a human point of view, it is possibly more necessary to mention the curses to deter a person from doing evil.

### 1. The Blessings (28:1–14)

The conditional promise is mentioned once more: If Israel would obey the Lord, He would set Israel above the nations of the earth and bless her (28:1–2). Once the Israelites accepted the Mosaic covenant and pledged allegiance to the Lord, they were assured of His blessings. But if the nation would not obey the Lord God and keep His commandments and decrees, then the nation could expect curses and judgments.

The blessings are written in the form of poetry that was recited as liturgy (28:3–6). Six blessings are mentioned—five short ones and one longer one (28:4). The blessings cover every aspect of a person's life: 1) Israel could expect all kinds of blessings—in the city, in the country, in every area of activity (28:3); 2) Israel would be blessed with children as well as an abundance of crops and livestock (28:4); 3) the nation would enjoy a surplus of food, the full basket and more than enough grain for bread (28:5); and 4) in summary, everything that an Israelite man or woman would seek to do, whether in or out of the house, God promised to abundantly bless (28:6).

Moses now expounds on the blessings that would affect every phase of life (28:7–14). Any enemy that would threaten Israel would run away in seven directions (28:7). God would defend Israel against them all. God's people would be blessed so abundantly that they would have more than enough to lend to poorer nations. Under no circumstances was Israel to borrow from any nation, thereby putting herself under an enemy's thumb (28:12b–13a). In fact, God's blessings would be so abundant that it would be difficult to store all the grain; the seasonal rains would make possible an abundant provision of crops (28:8, 11–12a).

The reason for the blessings is that the Lord called Israel

---

[36]Thompson, *Deuteronomy*, p. 268.

and established her on the basis of His oath. If God's people would only love Him and keep His commandments, then the nations of the earth would surely see and be in awe of the special relationship between God and Israel and realize that this nation is called by the name of the Lord (1 Sam. 15:29; Deut. 2:25; 11:25).

Finally, Israel is reminded to pay attention to God's commands and follow them, not going to the right or to the left, not serving other gods or goddesses to derive blessings from them. The Lord is the only one who would make the land fertile and bless the people abundantly (11:11–17).

### 2. The Curses (28:15–68; Hebrew 28:15–69)

**a. The Opposite of Blessings (28:15–19).** With the change of only a few minor words, the statement of curses (28:16–19) is given in a form almost exactly opposite to the blessings (28:3–6). Opening with a conditional statement, the Israelites are warned that if they did not follow all His commandments and statutes, then curses and God's judgments would come upon them. Six curses are mentioned, although they do not follow the same order as the blessings listed previously: 28:16 corresponds to 28:3; 28:17 corresponds to 28:5; 28:18 corresponds to 28:4; 28:19 corresponds to 28:6; 28:25 corresponds to 28:7; 28:20 corresponds to 28:8.

**b. Drought and Sickness (28:20–24).** For those Israelites who would dare to disobey the Lord and break the covenant, God would bring calamity, both on them and eventually on the entire nation, promising them curses, confusion, and rebuke. Disobedient Israel would go into a panic when her enemies would attack her.

God also reminds the Israelites that if they would ever make the gods of the foreign nations the object of their worship, He would send the plague upon them. The presence of disease was designed to be a sign that something was wrong between God and His people (28:21). Seven diseases are mentioned, attacking both the people and their plants and crops (28:22). Four diseases affected people: 1) wasting diseases, accompanied with a high fever; 2) fever, probably malaria; 3) inflammation (literally, "burning"), because some diseases are accompanied by a high

fever; and 4) a scorching heat or severe irritation on parts of the
body or inner organs, accompanied also with a high fever.

Three diseases affected plants and crops: 1) drought and not
sword (NASB), because a number of sources link scorching heat
and drought;[37] 2) blight, referring to the effects of the hot, desert
wind which drove up the temperature, lowered the humidity,
and caused the crops to die; and 3) mildew. The diseases which
attacked plants occurred when God simply shut off the seasonal
rains. The sky became like bronze, the sun shone, no clouds
were in sight, and every plant dried up. The ground likewise
became as hard as iron (similar wording appears in the Esarhaddon treaties, describing the same kind of weather conditions in
the Middle East).[38] The Deuteronomic treaty is unique because
Israel's disobedience would prompt her God-King to diminish
the rain supply, causing the ground to either become dry as iron
or fine and powdery. When the ground became dusty, the
blowing wind would fill the air with it, making living conditions
miserable. The condition of the land was designed to be a
barometer of the spiritual relationships between God and His
people. When the land brought forth abundance, it was a sign of
a high spiritual level in Israel. But drought conditions reflected
a spiritual breakdown, and the nation was warned to return to
the Lord.

   c. **Diseases, Defeat, Disgrace, and Death (28:25–37).** Israel's disloyalty will cause them to be defeated by their enemies
(Lev. 26:17), but God's people will suffer even more. Their
defeat will be great as they scatter into seven different directions. Pagan nations will shudder because of what the Lord will
do to His people (Jer. 15:4; 24:9): 1) the bodies of dead Israelite
soldiers will lie on the ground, without even an honorable
burial; 2) their carcasses will be food for birds and beasts; and 3)
the few remnant Israelites will suffer even greater anguish.

   To emphasize that rebellion against the Lord was despi-
cable, Moses warned that God will punish rebellion with the
boils of Egypt (28:27). Unrepentant Israel will be treated like

---

[37] See the *New International Version* and *Jewish Publication Society of
America;* see also Craigie, *Deuteronomy,* p. 342 and Thompson, *Deuteronomy,*
p. 273.
[38] Thompson, *Deuteronomy,* p. 273.

the Egyptians! The rest of the diseases, tumors or ulcers, festering sores, and the itch will be further reminders of God's displeasure.

Judgment for disobedience also included emotional disturbances: madness, blindness, and confusion of the mind (literally, "terror of heart"). These were brought about either because of the severity of the skin diseases of 28:27 or because of deep despair. The people will grope as if they were blind, even in broad daylight. Whatever the Israelites planned will only end in disaster as they become prey for enemy nations, with no opportunity for rescue. Future prophets repeated these themes when subsequent generations had become disloyal to their God.

Dismay and horror will be heightened when enemies take whatever they want from Israel (28:30–33). An Israelite pledged to a wife might find that she had been snatched from him and raped by his enemies. When buildings were built and vineyards planted by those exempt from service, non-Israelites will take them instead (cf. 20:5–7). Oxen will be killed; donkeys, and sheep, will be taken away by enemy troops. Israel will become helpless in the face of God's punishments.

What has already been mentioned in 28:28–33 is now repeated, as if to emphasize that disloyalty and disobedience have a high price tag (28:34–37). These verses hint at a future exile, when Israelites will be confronted by the horror of their worship of the pagan gods; worst of all, Israel will be a horror, an object of scorn and ridicule. No doubt the pagan nations knew of the covenant relationship between Israel and the Lord, but they will only scoff and taunt Israel all the more, because He seems powerless to do anything for His people. The tragedy is that future generations did forget and suffered exile in Assyria and Babylon.

**d. A Faltering Economy and Forceable Exile (28:38–46).** Moses further describes the consequences of the curse. God will curse the harvest as well as the womb. Even though Israelites might work hard planting the field (28:38), cultivating vineyards (28:39), and tending olive trees (28:40), it will be to no avail. The locust will eat the crops, the worms will eat the grapes, and the olive trees will become diseased. In spite of all the hard work, there will be nothing to show for it. Children who usually helped on the farm will not be present to help their parents because foreign nations will take them into captivity.

Moses tells the people that the resident alien will prosper and will loan money to the Israelites, who will be poor, with no opportunity to repay their loans (the opposite of what is described in 28:12–13). Israel will no longer be favored, but rather became the tail of the nations. The curses are designed to be a sign and wonder, a warning to future generations to be sensitive to their covenant relationship (28:45–46).

**e. A Nation Degraded (28:47–57).** The prediction of horror for disobedience continues and becomes even more pointed. With the failure of rain, Israelites will be hungry, thirsty, and in dire poverty. They will become like animals with an iron yoke on their neck in their servanthood (28:47–48; Jer. 28:14). Their enemies will be fierce, having no respect for the elderly and no compassion for infants or children. Jeremiah used such language to describe the Babylonians (Jer. 5:15–17), and Habakkuk similarly described the Chaldeans (Hab. 1:6; or "Babylonians" as the NIV translates it). These foreign nations will apply a heavy tax on those who remained on the land, taking livestock, crops, grain, new wine, and oil. Little would be left, and Israel will be reduced to starvation (28:51).

Enemies will lay siege to Israelite cities (28:52), and even though the cities might be protected by high fortified walls, they will only be torn down. During the siege by enemies, food will become so scarce that Israelites will have to resort to cannibalism (28:53–55; 2 Kings 6:28–29), as indeed occurred during later sieges of Jerusalem. So serious will be these situations that even a gentle and sensitive woman will eat not only her newborn infant but the afterbirth as well, doing it in secret because she will not want to share with other members of her family (28:56–57). Moses was not engaged in mere rhetoric; he wanted to paint a picture of such horror that no future generation would ever want to rebel against the Lord.

**f. A Summary of God's Judgment (28:58–68; Hebrew 28:56–69).** Moses now summarizes the consequences of judgment because of the curses. He declares again that God would rather have Israel follow carefully the words revealed in Deuteronomy and have both reverence and love for the Lord

God. If the Israelites turned their backs on God, then they will experience His wrath. The word pictures in the summary may not be as horrible as the previous section, but the experiences will be real and difficult. Even as God judged Egypt with severe illnesses and caused their first-born to die, so Israel will suffer in the same way (28:58–61). Even though the rather small family of Jacob had grown to be a great nation and was favored of the Lord, yet in judgment their numbers will be diminished (28:62). While obedience results in life in the land of milk ánd honey, the curses will cause Israel to be exiled, and many Israelites will die in the land of their captivity (28:63).

A favored nation who would make the mistake of worshiping pagan gods will, in the exile, learn the horror of this worship. There she will have no rest in her soul; she will be anxious and weary, despair for her own safety, suffer severely, and be in constant suspense, filled with dread of day and night to suffer severely (28:65–67). Throughout the centuries when Israel was in exile, these very experiences became an actuality. Some Israelites will even be taken back to Egypt. But the irony was that Egyptians will not even want them as slaves (28:68). Moses painted a heartrending picture of what would happen to a people who, destined to be blessed of God, could end in tragedy.

**For Further Study**

1. Study how a number of commentators relate the details of covenant faith in 12:1–26:19 to the Decalogue.

2. Discuss the meaning of God's choice of sanctuary—wherever He places His name.

3. Discuss why Israel was to be so careful with the pagan worship of the people in the land they were to conquer.

4. What relevance do the dietary laws have for today?

5. Study the meaning of the one, two, or even three tithes.

6. Examine commentaries and source material to discover how the Middle Eastern treaties and codes provided for the poor.

7. What influence does the release from debt in Israel's Sabbatical have on Western society?

8. What hint do you see in the instructions for caring for slaves that slavery was to be abolished as an institution?

9. Trace in the Gospels the occurrence of the festivals described in Deuteronomy.

10. List God's conditions for Israel's king. Then examine the kings of Israel and Judah to discover who fulfilled these conditions and who violated them.

11. Study the words relating to the occult (18:9–14). Illustrate how Israel followed the occult practices.

12. Using Deuteronomy and the Mishnah tractate Sanhedrin (H. Danby, p. 382ff.) as your sources, compare each document's rules for determining evidence that could convict a possible murderer.

13. Study Israel's exemptions for service in war and the possible reasons for exemption today.

14. Compare Deuteronomy's guidelines for military hygiene in Israel and army practice today.

15. Compare Deuteronomy's guidelines for marriage and divorce with what Jesus taught.

16. Compare Deuteronomy's guidelines for charging interest with what was being charged in the Middle Eastern nations of that period.

17. Compare Deuteronomy's instructions for caring for the mother bird with what is recommended by the humane societies today.

18. Examine and list the various passages that deal with how Israel was to care for the poor. How do these guidelines relate to how we should care for the poor and needy today?

19. What is the correlation between the covenant blessings and curses and the New Testament guidelines for the behavior of believers?

# Chapter 4

## The Third Address:
## An Appeal for the Covenant

(Deuteronomy 29:1–30:20; Hebrew 28:68–30:20)

Commentators are uncertain whether 29:1 (Hebrew 28:68) is a conclusion of the preceding chapters of covenant renewal or whether it is the introduction to Moses' third address. The phrase "the terms of the covenant" does serve as a fitting end to chapters 5–28. However, this statement along with 29:9 can also serve well as the introduction to Moses' third address. Perhaps the connection between verses 1 and 2 is the same as the connection between 4:45 and 5:1, where the former is a transition to 5:1. Verse 1 could also be a transition to verse 2, making an introduction to the third address.

Moses' address summed up what he already had presented in the previous chapters, following the pattern of the Middle Eastern treaties: 1) reviewing what God did for Israel in the past; 2) challenging Israel to receive the covenant offered by God; 3) reviewing the curses of the covenant, and 4) dealing with the possibility of restoration even after the curses and judgments (chap. 30).

### A. An Appeal to Be Faithful (29:1–29; Hebrew 28:69–29:29)

#### 1. Reviewing the Past (29:1–8)

As the mediator of the covenant (1:1; 4:44), Moses continues to expand and explain the covenant of Exodus 19–24.

Moses narrates again Israel's past experiences in Egypt and the wilderness, describing God's great miraculous signs and wonders. The older members of the second generation remembered these experiences, while the much younger ones had heard of them over and over again (29:2–3). Moses told this second generation that even though they had managed to get to the east bank of the Jordan, they did not actually comprehend God's great deeds (29:4); their eyes did not see, neither did their ears hear. Moses no doubt challenged his people to listen and understand with their hearts so that they would be able spiritually to discern what God was saying. Merely winning victories because of an intellectual assent to God's directives was not enough; the Lord wanted a total heart commitment from His people. Closed and hard hearts are ever a problem, both in Old and New Testaments (Isa. 6:9ff.; 2 Cor. 3:12–15).

In verse 5 the pronoun changes to "I" as if to accentuate that Moses, as God's representative, led the Israelites through the desert, and they had no reason to complain: clothes and sandals had not worn out; they had eaten no bread made by human hands but had been fed with manna from heaven (29:5); they had not drunk of any fermented drink, but instead, the water had come miraculously from the rock (8:3); finally the second generation had arrived on the east bank. Moses describes again how Sihon and Og had been defeated, and their land on the east bank had been taken as an inheritance for Reuben, Gad, and a half-tribe of Manasseh (29:7; 2:33–20; 3). In a fitting conclusion, the Lord speaks through Moses and challenges Israel to know Him in a spiritual sense. Only in the first-hand relationship with Him, only in truly knowing Him could Israel enjoy His spiritual blessings.

## 2. A Call to Commitment (29:9–21)

Moses reminds the Israelites that the terms of the covenant must be ever before them; as they took these directives to heart, they would be enabled to do what the Word required in order that they could prosper (29:9). Moses must have given this call to remember on a special occasion because the people were standing before the presence of the Lord—tribal leaders first, elders, officials, and then the men of Israel with their children and wives, along with the aliens and servants (29:10–11; Josh. 8:35; 24:1; 1 Sam. 10:19).

The ratification of the covenant was a solemn occasion (29:12). God had called Israel (first Abraham and now as a nation), and He took on Himself the responsibility to care for His people (29:12–13). But Israel was to respond to the covenant through the sealing of the oath (literally, "curse," from the Hebrew ' *ala*). Once Israel accepted the covenant, she would then be held responsible for her allegiance to Him. If she should rebel, she would also experience the oaths of the covenant mentioned in the previous two chapters, and judgment would come upon the nation. Each generation must understand God's mercy and love and realize God is faithful. But again, every generation must in its own way respond in love, be loyal, and yield its allegiance to God in order to experience His blessings.

Moses again recalls the experiences in Egypt and the wilderness where the people had been exposed to many pagan worship systems, and images and idols of wood, stone, silver, and gold (29:16–17). Two lessons became paramount: 1) the pagan worship systems are detestable, an abomination to the Lord. The gods of the nations are nothing more than vain human imaginations, but for Israel to worship them would be nothing less than an affront to God; 2) Israel was to remember the Lord's great saving acts and realize that He is the one to serve. The Israelites were never to turn from the God of Israel and worship false gods (29:18). If the people should persist in doing what Moses had warned against, allowing the root of false worship to grow in the heart, they would hear the words of the oath (curse, '*ala*). Some might bless themselves as they worshiped false gods, thinking they were safe (29:19). If this mockery persisted, the end result will be judgment in accordance with the curses. And the names of the rebellious people will be blotted out, to be forgotten eternally (29:20). The Lord will apprehend the sinner out of the midst of the multitudes and judge the sinner in accordance with the curses of the covenant (29:21). Subsequent generations often played the harlot with pagan gods and goddesses, only to suffer the curses mentioned in the previous chapter. Believers today often think they can get away with half-hearted worship and at the same time court the gods of this world: money, success, power, and prestige. Moses' warnings to Israel are still relevant today.

### 3. Teach, Teach, and Teach (29:22-29)

Moses now describes what would happen to the Israelites if God would have to judge them. Rebellious Israelites would see their land a waste, and in the midst of their calamities and diseases, they will ruefully ask why the Lord had permitted His land to become such a waste and why His burning anger rests on them.

In his role as teacher, Moses proclaims to this future generation that they had abandoned the covenant relationship. In what sense had Israel abandoned the Lord? The rebellion that Moses foresees is described succinctly: they will adopt the pagan gods—bow down to them, worship them—and thereby prostitute the worship of the real God. That is why the land will be devastated and why some will even go into exile. The children of Israel were to ever remember Moses' vivid explanation of what will happen to people who decide that they are more clever than God Himself. It is no less true today among God's people. The warning is ever before each of us: it is not how well we begin; the measure of faithfulness is always how well we end.

The lesson is plain. Each generation was to carefully teach its children, and encourage them to enter into the covenant God had with Israel. The fathers were always held responsible to make sure that children also learn what the Lord has provided, thereby enabling them to love Him as their God. The truth for today within the body of Christ is that God reveals His secret things in His Word so that we can know Him and experience His blessings (29:29).

## B. Encouragement to Make the Right Decisions (30:1-20)

Moses already had told the people of the solemn consequences of disobedience and the ultimate judgment of exile to foreign lands. But even as God in His mercy and grace provided a covenant to Israel, so now He makes provision that if a remnant of Israelites in a foreign land will realize that they were suffering because of their own wrongdoing, they could also be restored.

### 1. The Promise of Restoration (30:1–10)

If a remnant of Israel will repent, then God will also move in the circumstances to recover and establish them in the land. The covenant will then be ratified again so that the remnant could enter into His blessings (30:1–2). The verb "return" *(shuv)* is very important. While Israel might turn away, Moses and the prophets always held out the possibility that a remnant could also turn around to once more face the Lord and acknowledge Him as their God (see 4:29–30).

If a repentant remnant would turn, the Lord would "restore your fortunes" (literally, "turn your turnings"). The point is that if the nation will turn away from the Lord, He will have no recourse but to judge that nation as outlined in the curses. But if they should turn to face the Lord, then He Himself will change His attitude and their fortune will also be changed (29:3–5). The situation today is a bit different in modern Israel because while so many of the people have already returned to their land, most are still agnostic. This might be a special situation whereby God will eventually turn the nation *in their own land* instead of in exile. One day all Israel will turn to Him in repentance (Ezek. 36:24–36; 37:23–28; Rom. 11:25–27).

For the remnant that will return, God will also circumcise their hearts (30:6; 10:16). We must not see a contradiction between 10:16 and this passage. In 10:16, the people were told to circumcise their hearts, but 30:6 emphasizes that God will regenerate the heart so that people will truly know Him. Both dimensions are necessary: the person needs to repent, but God changes the heart.

When Israel will be restored and many know the Lord, then the curses that once rested on an unrepentant Israel will come on the heads of Israel's enemies (30:7). The Lord will then make His people prosperous in all that they will do, giving them many children and abundant livestock and crops (30:3, 9; 28:3–6). God will take delight in His people as they will once again be responsible in their covenant relationship (30:10).

## 2. Choose Life (30:11–16)

Moses challenges this second generation to choose life. A single nod of the head affirmatively or a shaking of the head in a negative manner could lead to either blessing or cursing. A decision by the second generation was not difficult or beyond their reach. God was ready to enable His people to serve Him and do for them beyond what they could even ask or think. It is the same case today; God will never send anyone to a task without preparation. By His grace and mercy, God's people can serve Him with great power.

Moses reminds the people that what they were being asked to do was not lost somewhere in the heavens. Someone did not have the difficult assignment of going there, obtaining God's directives, and then returning to proclaim it to the people (30:12). Neither was the commandment lost somewhere out at sea. No one had to go on a perilous voyage to obtain it and bring it back to God's people (30:13). Both of these phrases, "ascending to heaven" and setting out to "cross the sea to look for" a revelation or a person, also appear in other Middle Eastern literature.[1]

Moses declares that the word of revelation was near—in their mouths and in their hearts; they need only be responsible for and obey what God already had revealed. God's people are not expected to know everything there is to know (29:29), but they are to be responsible for what is near at hand (4:6-8; Ps. 19:7–11; 119). Only as we obey what we do know will additional revelation be given to us.

Paul used this terminology in his appeal to his people (Rom. 10:6–8). Many had become too involved with an altogether too human interpretation of the Word of God. Addressing their doubts, Paul told them that the righteous Messiah was at hand, and they would not find it difficult to believe in Him.

Moses presents the people with the choice: life and prosperity or death and destruction (30:15). In strong language, Moses commands them to love the Lord, walk in His ways, and highly regard and value His commands, decrees, and laws. To

---

[1] Craigie, *Deuteronomy*, p. 365.

choose life was to choose the Promised Land and then, with a resolute heart, lay hold on everything God has.

### 3. Turn From Death (30:17–20)

Making wrong decisions has consequences. The second generation was warned against making wrong choices. The alternative was sobering: God would become their enemy and, as has already been indicated in the curses, rebels could only look forward to being destroyed and cut off from the commonwealth of Israel (30:17–18).

In the Middle Eastern treaties, the call for witnesses was very common, and even the phrase "heaven and earth" was used as one of the witnesses.[2] The witness from heaven was God Himself, while earth testified on behalf of creation (4:26; Mic. 6:1–2). The idea of calling God to witness Israel's decision was to be a strong deterrent against making wrong choices. The encouragement was to choose life, love the Lord, listen to Him, and cling to Him.

### For Further Study

1. Search through the Old Testament and find the occasions when the covenant was renewed, either from generation to generation, or from spiritual renewal to spiritual renewal.

2. Review Old Testament history to find when spiritual renewal took place or when a remnant realized their sinfulness and turned back to the Lord to renew the covenant.

3. Explain in detail how Paul adapted 30:11–14 for his purposes.

---

[2]Thompson, *Deuteronomy*, p. 287.

# Chapter 5

## Moses' Last Words and His Death
(Deuteronomy 31:1–34:12)

Moses' three major messages were finished at the end of chapter 30. The last four chapters of Deuteronomy treat the personal matters relating to his approaching death: He charges Joshua with leadership, completes the covenant, and puts it into the ark as a most appropriate and sacred place. Even while he cares for these details, he continues to warn Israel about her responsibility to the covenant relationship. God will give him opportunity to see the land from afar and then bless the tribes of Israel. And in a last will and testament, he will describe his own personal walk with God as well as further warn Israel in his song (chap. 32). The final chapter, added to Deuteronomy no doubt as a postscript by Joshua, provides the details about Moses' death.

### A. The Law and Joshua (31:1–29)

#### 1. Encouragement by Moses and Presentation of Joshua (31:1–8)

Again, commentators question whether verse 1 is a continuation of chapter 30 (making chap. 30–33 a unit) or whether verse 1 introduces the remaining chapters as a separate unit. It seems that Moses' messages are contained in chapters 1–30, while the transition in leadership and preparation for departure should be a separate unit in chapters 31–33. Joshua has already been mentioned in 1:38 and 3:28, but Moses gives further guidelines to Joshua in preparation for his pending leadership.

Moses is now one hundred twenty years old and no longer

as active as he once was, not able to "lead you" (31:2). He had lived long enough to see grown grandchildren. He was indeed the elder statesman to the nation, but he also had to confess that God had told him he would not cross the Jordan River with the second generation and their children. Moses emphasizes again that Israel's God is the Lord, the commander-in-chief who would lead Israel into the Promised Land, destroy the nations before them, and enable them to take possession of the land (31:3). Joshua would be the tactical general, taking his orders from the Lord. And just as God had overthrown Sihon and Og, along with their troops, so He would deliver the pagan nations and their leaders into Israel's hands (31:4). Moses reminds them not to forget the stipulations of war in destroying these nations (31:5). He encourages Israel and Joshua to be strong and courageous (31:6, 7, 23; Josh. 1:6–9, 18). They were not to be afraid because the presence of God will assure His people of victory.

While Joshua had already been set apart before the congregation (1:38; Num. 27:18–23), Moses now summons him to stand in the presence of all Israel, where he charges Joshua with the leadership responsibility (31:7). Even as the Lord had been with Moses, so He would also be with Joshua, enabling him to carry out exactly what had already been outlined: conquer the land and divide it for the inheritance of Israel. Moses tells Joshua not to be afraid; God, the commander-in-chief, would give him the battle plans (31:8).

## 2. The Sabbatical Reading of the Law (31:9–13)

Ratification of the Middle Eastern treaties required that the documents regularly be read in public. Likewise, after the law-covenant was committed to writing, Moses (representing the Lord) handed a copy to the priest-leaders for safekeeping in the sanctuary. No doubt, Joshua also had a copy (31:9).

Moses commands the priests to read the law to the people every seventh year (the Sabbatical) during the Feast of Tabernacles when representatives of all Israel appeared before the Lord (31:10–11; 15:1ff.; 16:13–15). (Israel was instructed to appear at a place designated by the Lord, but in time, this would be Jerusalem.) It is questionable whether every Israelite was

able to come for this special occasion. Possibly, representative
heads of families and family members on a rotating basis would
somehow make the trip to at least one of the three pilgrimage
festivals in the course of a year, but as many as possible would
try to be at the central sanctuary during the Sabbatical Feast of
Tabernacles.

Moses gives detailed instructions for the people to listen, to
learn, and to fear the Lord the God of Israel. The assembly was
to include men, women, and children, as well as the aliens
living in Israel (31:12). It was extremely necessary that every
new generation would become acquainted with the covenant
relationship so that each could yield allegiance to the God of
Israel. As the generations would come and go, they would listen
to the covenant and then try to do what God asked them to do to
establish a continual living relationship with the Lord.

### 3. The Charge to Moses and Joshua (31:14–29)

These verses describe three events: 1) Moses commissions
Joshua as a continuation of what had already been mentioned in
31:6–8; 2) he warns Israel to yield allegiance to the Lord of the
covenant, especially in view of future disobedience and disaster; and 3) he then emphasizes the testimony of the Law.

a. **Joshua Is Set Apart (31:14–15, 23).** What had been public
in setting Joshua apart now becomes a private meeting between
the Lord, Moses, and Joshua. While Israel's leadership and
people knew that Joshua was to take Moses' position, it was
necessary now to have the sense of God's intimate commission-
ing as a further encouragement to the new leader when he
would serve in the place of Moses (31:14). As the two were in
the tent, the presence of the Lord appeared in the pillar of cloud
over the tent entrance as a sign to everyone that a private
meeting was in progress. God commands Joshua to accept the
responsibility; He encourages him to be strong and courageous,
for he would lead Israel across the Jordan River and into the
Promised Land. The Lord assures Joshua that He would go
before to clear the way (31:23).

b. **Possible Disaster and Preparation of a Warning
(31:16–22).** Moses' career was a long one. He spent the first
forty years of his life learning Egyptian culture as well as the

cultures of other peoples with whom Egypt had diplomatic relationships. During his second forty years he lived in the back side of the desert, where he humbled himself before the Lord. But he also came to know the Sinai Peninsula well. Finally, when he was eighty years old, he became God's man to lead two generations of Israelites for another forty years. Now on the east bank of the Jordan River he is about to surrender his leadership. He had been faithful to the Lord, delivering the law to Israel, expounding it, and encouraging the people to choose life and blessings and avoid the curses and death. Now, on the verge of passing from this scene, he is told that "these people will soon prostitute themselves to the foreign gods of the land they are entering" (31:16). What was the response in Moses' heart to this word? He knew human nature could easily turn a people away from God and cause them to be disloyal to the covenant. God did not declare that rebellion would happen immediately, but He informed Moses that He also knew what was in the human heart. When people become disloyal, His curses will become an actuality. When the anger of the Lord arises, He will turn away from His people, and they will suffer disaster and difficulty as a result of their disobedience (31:17–18).

God told His servant therefore to prepare a song which would serve as a warning to the Israelites (31:19). The song was to reflect some of Moses' tremendous experiences with the Lord, but it would also contain a warning to the people. When they sang it, they would remember that if they turned away from God, He would turn from them (31:21). The song would remind them that after enjoying a prosperity made possible because of God's graciousness, they would be sinning greatly to turn from Him. This song was to be so well known that it would always be a witness against rebellious and stubborn people. Moses then wrote the words of the song (31:22), which is presented in 31:30–32:47, while someone else set it to music, perhaps at a later date.

**c. Testimony of the Law (31:24–29).** Some difficulty may be apparent as to what is meant by "the words of this law" (31:24) and "Book of the Law" (31:26) which was to be given to the Levites. The Levites, in turn, were to put it beside the ark of the covenant of the Lord as a witness against Israel. Since the

Decalogue tablet was placed inside the ark (Exod. 25:16), the question is whether "the words" refers to chapters 5 to 28 which were given to the priests to be read to Israel on the Sabbatical year (31:9–13), or whether this phrase refers to the song which Moses was to prepare as a testimony to Israel. It would appear from the context, beginning with 31:19, that this phrase refers to the song which will be Israel's constant reminder to be continually committed to the Lord their God. Future generations will never be able to say they had not been forewarned against their tendency to rebel against the Lord.

Moses now calls together the tribal elders as well as other officials for the purpose of sharing his song. He wanted to impress on them the responsibility of leadership (31:28). In order to emphasize his concern, he once more calls on the witnesses of heaven and earth to testify against the leaders as in a courtroom scene where charges on behalf of God are brought against the elders as defendants. Moses was well aware that after he died, future generations will become utterly corrupt and turn from God's revelation, bringing on themselves the curses of the covenant (31:29). The elders first heard the song and then were charged with the responsibility to share it with the entire congregation and with every succeeding generation.

## B. Moses' Song (31:30–32:47)

The introduction to Moses' song is in prose form (31:30), while the song itself is in poetic form (chap. 32). Verse 30 tells us that Moses recited the words of the song to the whole assembly (the music to the song was introduced at a later date). One can imagine the strong impact the words (and music) could have had on the listeners. The setting was designed to remind the people of their covenant relationship with their God and to encourage them to be faithful to His commandments and statutes.

Another interesting feature of this song is its literary form, which follows the pattern of the Middle Eastern treaties between suzerain leaders and their subject-vassals. The pattern followed in these treaties is known as the *riv* or legal suit pattern.[1] The subdivisions of the song reflect the different parts of the treaty. The song, therefore, is a lawsuit itself, reflecting the covenant relationship as a very important witness between God and His people. The treaty form is not followed exactly, but Moses adapted it for his own purposes, as we shall note.

### 1. Introduction (32:1–4)

The heavens and earth are called as witnesses to hear the Lord's indictment of His people (see 30:19; 31:28). Every time the covenant was renewed, Israelites were reminded to be responsible in their relationship with the Lord and listen to Moses' teaching (32:1–2). Even as the rain, dew, showers, and abundant rain were necessary for vegetation, so the teaching and words of God were also refreshing to the listener (32:2). The Land of Promise was dependent on the rain which came from God; likewise the people Israel were to be completely depen- dent on the word and instructions of the covenant.

The poetry of Moses' song at the crossing of the Sea of Reeds (Exod. 15:1–18) is more rapid, with shorter lines. But here, with "words" and "teaching" that are associated with the wisdom literature, the lines are longer. Moses chose the longer lines, which take additional time to sing, in order to impress the truths of the covenant on the Israelite's hearts.

Moses calls on the Israelites to lay hold of faith whereby they could trust and proclaim the sacred name of the Lord (32:3a) and His many attributes (32:3b–4). Moses reminds the people that the God of Israel is great, and He is to be praised (32:3b). He is the Rock, suggesting that He can be trusted because He is steadfast in every situation (32:13; see also 32:15, 18, 30–31). The works of God are perfect, and His ways are just (32:4b). He is also faithful (which is also one of His names, *'aman*), and in no way can He do wrong. The God of Israel is also upright and just. In perfectly balanced Hebrew poetic parallelism, Moses ascribes his praise to the God he knows. But beyond a personal hymn of praise, this song is also a call for Israel to know Him personally.

---

[1] Thompson, *Deuteronomy*, p. 295.

## 2. A Complaint (32:5–6)

In contrast to God's great faithfulness, many in Israel will become faithless and rebellious. Following the pattern of the *riv* lawsuit, Moses, on behalf of the Lord-King, brings a complaint against His rebellious subjects.

Unlike the Rock, Israel had the tendency to be corrupt, and a future generation will become warped, crooked, and shameful to behold (32:5). But the complaint becomes all the more pointed: Is this the way you repay the Lord? Why play the part of fools (the worst possible kind was the example of Nabal in 1 Sam. 25:1–39) and be people who are not wise at all? Will another generation forget that God originally called the Israelites, brought them out of Egypt, and entered into a covenant relationship with them at Mount Horeb? Could the Israelites have any existence apart from the God who made and formed them? It was a serious complaint, and any generation that fit this description will be in serious danger (32:5).

## 3. The Mighty Acts of a Faithful God (32:7–14)

Again paralleling the pattern of the lawsuit, Moses recites the benevolent acts of the Suzerain toward His subject-vassals. He asks the people to "remember the days of old" (32:7), to recall the history of God's goodness. He tells the children to ask their fathers and their elders to explain their history. Moses then lists God's specific acts for Israel in the past.

First, the Most High had established the nations and had given each one their inheritance, setting up their boundaries. This is the only passage in Deuteronomy that uses the name "Most High" (*'elyon*), suggesting that He is sovereign over the nations and has the right to fix their boundaries. The last line in 32:8 is interesting; the Hebrew textual reading is "sons of Israel" but the Septuagint and a Qumran fragment from Cave 4 read "sons of God." If the latter is correct, then a beautiful contrast is suggested that wherein the Most High is sovereign over the nations, yet He is the one who gave Jacob and his sons, the sons of God, their allotted inheritance in the Land of Promise (32:9).

Second, He had established Israel in their fixed inheritance, calling His people out of Egypt, leading them through the desert. Moses uses three images to describe how the Lord had taken care of His people (32:10–12): 1) He had been the kindly Father who carefully tended His people, regarding them as the pupil, the precious part of His eye; 2) He had been like the mother eagle who, when she is ready to teach her young how to fly, starts breaking up the nest in order to push them out of it; at the same time she spreads her wings underneath as a support to help her eaglets make their first faltering attempts to fly; and 3) the Lord had led His people through the wilderness as a shepherd, providing them with whatever they needed. Moses emphasizes that He had been the only one to serve Israel; no foreign or pagan god would have cared to do it.

Third, God would lead them to "the heights of the land," the Land of Promise (32:13). There they would have everything in abundance: the fruit of the crops and the trees, honey, olive oil, curds (butter), milk, the finest meat, wheat, and wine (32:14). In view of such an expression of grace and love, how could some future generation, to their shame, exchange the mighty acts of their God, the Lord, for the emptiness of worthless pagan gods?

### 4. The Indictment Against an Apostate People (32:15–18)

The title "Jeshurun," a pet name (literally, "the upright one," 33:5, 26; Isa. 44:2), is contrasted to what will come from the hearts of a future generation who, having had every material blessing, will become apostate. A generation to come—fat, filled with food, heavy and sleek—will have the audacity to turn away from truth, abandoning the God who made them. They will reject their Rock and choose instead the foreign, pagan, abominable idols, even sacrificing to the demons. The word "demons" (*shedim*), occurring only here and in Psalm 106:37, refers to so-called gods which these generations of Israel had not known; but Moses speaks here of future generations who will become acquainted with them.

### 5. The Judgment (32:19–25)

In response to such rebellion, the Lord will be angry and shield His face because of what He must do in accordance with the curses (32:19). He is the God of love, but with such emotions stirred up because of stiff-necked and rebellious people, He had no recourse but to judge them (32:20).

To emphasize the horror of it all, Moses uses a play on words which mocks such reprobates (32:21). A rebellious people worshiped that which is no-god (*lo' 'el*), and as a result, they will experience God's judgment by those who are no-people (*lo' 'am*). Once judgment came on Israel, they will cry out to the no-god, but no answer will come to deliver the nation from the no-people who have "no understanding" (literally, "a foolish nation"). So great will be God's wrath that it will extend to the depths of Sheol, where the dead are located. And His fire will devour the earth and its harvest and even set on fire the foundation of the mountains. The land of Israel will be devastated exactly according to the curses of chapter 28: famine, diseases, wild beasts, siege against the cities, and finally, death (32:23–25). The New Testament similarly pictures God's wrath: "It is a dreadful thing to fall into the hands of the living God," and "Our God is a consuming fire" (Heb. 10:31; 12:29).

## 6. God's Mournful Discourse (32:26–38)

At this point, Moses adapted the usual lawsuit pattern. Instead of continuing to describe what a suzerain-king would do in judgment against a rebellious people, he describes a compassionate God who would only cry plaintively for His people. He was ready to bless His people if they would only turn from their ways.

God seems to plead with a mournful and rueful note: "I said I will scatter them . . . but" (32:26–27). He contemplates what Israel's enemies would say of Israel; this was a factor in withholding His judgment. God is ever careful to protect His own glory, and He did not want Israel's enemies to claim that their strength brought about Israel's destruction. These enemies would learn, sooner or later, that their victory over Israel was only because God *permitted* it and not because they had the power to win their own battles (see also 9:28; Isa. 48:9–11; Ezek. 20:9, 14, 22; etc.).

God further assesses the apostate generation: they are without sense; they have no discernment (32:28). Were they not

clever enough to realize He meant what He said that if people
were disobedient, His curses will come down on them? A nation
is never so blind as when it will not listen (32:29)! Did not God
protect His people in the past? But now the situation is
different. Could not the people understand the reason why one
enemy soldier put one thousand Israelites to flight and two
could put ten thousand into a panic? Did they not realize that
the Rock of Israel will turn against them because of their
disobedience (32:30)?

Moses continues by mocking the pagan gods who were no-
rock at all (32:31). Surprisingly, many enemy leaders did
concede they were only operating within the permissive will of
Israel's God to execute His judgment (Exod. 14:25; Josh.
2:9–10; 1 Sam. 4:8; 5:7–12; etc.). However, Israel's enemies
were evil, like Sodom and Gomorrah, and their only offer to the
apostates will be poison, bitterness, the venom of serpents, and
poison of cobras (32:32–33). Apostate Israel must learn first-
hand that while the pomp and glory of the pagan nations seem
enticing, their vain gifts will in the end only lead to destruction.

The words "in reserve" and "sealed" describe the secret
purposes of God when, in due time, He will take action against
Israel's enemies when a remnant of His people will repent
(32:34–35). God will use Israel's enemies to pressure His
people; in the end He will judge these very enemies for their
immoral acts. (In one such future instance, God permitted
Babylon to attack Israel, taking many into exile; but He brought
judgment against this wicked nation once a remnant of His
exiled people were purified [Jer. 51:45–58].) But God will not
act until the rebellious generation will suffer severely, with no
strength left, and after many had died (32:36). In their extremity
they will realize that the so-called rocks (gods) of enemy nations
are only useless. The Lord will even taunt His suffering people,
asking them to call on the false gods to help them and give them
shelter (32:37–38). The purpose of exile and suffering was that
one day at least a remnant will realize that their foolishness only
gave them grief.

### 7. The Promise of Deliverance (32:39–42)

God promised deliverance to a purified remnant because He alone is God; they were to understand this basic truth and know that no pagan god could stand beside Him (32:39). He has both the power to put people to death as well as to restore people and give them life. He wounds, but He can also heal.

Moses pictures God as lifting His hand to take an oath in the courtroom: "As surely as I live forever" (32:40). God gave His word that He will deliver the remnant, based on His name. Once God begins to act, none of the enemy nations who dared to attack an apostate generation of Israel will be able to stand. God's flashing sword will act in judgment against His adversaries (Israel's enemies) with a terrible vengeance. And He will repay the leaders of the enemy nations (32:41–42). A purified remnant will once again realize who their God is and enter once more into the covenant relationship, yielding allegiance to Him. Each generation had to learn that it was far better to accept the godly lifestyle of the covenant than to learn by bitter experience the judgment of His curses.

### 8. A Call to Worship (32:43)

The end of Moses' song is a call to the nations, along with Israel, to rejoice in the Lord. God is the Victor, and He knows how to care for His people, restore a remnant, and care for enemy nations who would attack His people. When the enemies are defeated, when the guilt of Israel is cleared away, and when His people are forgiven, then there is cause for Israel and the nations who remain to sing the praises of the true God, the Lord of Israel. One day, in a prophetic sense, when all of Israel and the remaining nations will know the Lord, they will both rejoice together in the kingdom (Ps. 22:22–31).

### 9. Take Care How You Listen (32:44–47)

After Moses and Joshua speak the words of the song to the people, they ask them to "take to heart all the words" (32:46). Not only the people but also their children were to be responsible to the covenant relationship. The song was not meant to be mere words, but instead the words were life indeed.

## C. Moses Sees the Land and Blesses the Tribes (32:48–33:29)

### 1. Preparation for Death (32:48–52)

Moses now comes to the end of his earthly ministry, and the Lord directs him to ascend Mount Nebo, which was a mountain peak in the Abarim range, east of the north end of the Dead Sea. From that vantage point he was able to see the land that he was not permitted to enter (3:25–27). Remember that Moses was not allowed to enter the Promised Land because: 1) on one occasion he was supposed to speak to the rock for water to come forth, but instead he struck it twice (Num. 20:1–12); and 2) he had responded in anger to the people, saying, "Listen, you rebels, must we bring you water out of this rock?" Instead of explaining that the Lord was going to provide water for His people, Moses in his wrath had exploded and implied that he could provide the water (Num. 20:10; see also Ps. 106:32–33). Lest one feel that this is punishment beyond the actual offense, we must realize that no leader can afford to wrongly interpret God's intentions or he will give excuse to those who want to rebel against the Lord and go their way. It is a solemn responsibility for God's servants to be sensitive to His desires and wishes so that His people will know exactly what is His word. Yet, God was gracious in allowing Moses to see the entire land from Mount Nebo.

### 2. Blessing the Tribes (33:1–29)

We are not told when Moses delivered this blessing. He may have done so after he delivered his song and before he ascended to the mount. He spoke on behalf of God and blessed the tribes.

Like Moses' song, the blessings are in poetic form. They were recited, or possibly sung, at the close of the ceremony of the covenant renewal. Note the military motif in many of the lines, suggesting that Moses anticipated the great victory that would be wrought in the Promised Land. He himself, to the very end, spoke on a note of triumph, as seen in the last section. An era was passing as Moses closed out his own career on the east bank.

Scholars question whether Moses or a later editor wrote

these first five verses. Craigie suggests that verses 3b–5 may have been a "response made by the assembled people to Moses' initial words."[2] Even though the suggestion could be questioned, it possibly helps the reader understand verse 4. However, an editor could have added the opening verse that calls Moses the man of God, and explains that he pronounced the blessings on the tribes before his death.

The blessings are initiated on a note of praise (33:2), and they end in the same way (33:26–29). Moses recalls how the Lord met with Israel at Mount Sinai (used only in Deuteronomy for Mount Horeb) and shone on them like the sun from Mount Seir and Mount Paran (see Judg. 5:4–5). The three points suggest possibly the movement of Israel in the desert and how God protected them along the way. The heavenly hosts were with the Lord as well. The phrase "mountain slopes" evidently refers to some area in the Sinai, Ribeboth-Kodesh, although these areas are not known today.

The nation next seemingly responds, recognizing that Moses gave the law to Israel (33:3b–5). Moses was the mediator, representing God as the King over Jeshurun, the upright one, which was a favored name God bestowed on His people (32:15). Israel was a theocracy, with the Lord as King, and even though the name "Lord" does not appear in the text, nevertheless one cannot escape the fact that He has the right to exercise kingship over His people.

The blessings now follow (at times it will be difficult to sense the meaning of various passages). Each tribe was introduced with a short phrase in prose but the blessing itself appears in poetic form.

REUBEN (33:6). What Jacob had once said about Reuben was hardly complimentary (Gen. 49:3–4), but Moses blessed the people of Reuben, saying that they should live and not die. Even though the tribe was unstable because they found it difficult to be ready when military action was necessary (Judg. 5:15–16), they were blessed anyway.

JUDAH (33:7). What the blessing for this tribe means is not clear. The Targum Onkelos paraphrases the first two lines to

---

[2]Craigie, *Deuteronomy*, p. 392

read, "Hear, O Lord, the prayer of Judah when he goes into battle, and bring him back in peace." Does this mean that Judah was reckoned as the head of the tribes as it led Israel into battle? If this was the case, then Judah was in a responsible position, and the prayer was that God would listen and would enable their military troops to return safely to their families. Even though the people of Judah might have to fight with their own hands, the Lord would battle on their behalf and preserve them.

An interesting point emerges: in Moses' entire blessing, the tribe of Simeon is not mentioned at all. Simeon's inheritance was to be scattered among Israel (Gen. 49:7) and in the allotment of the tribal territories, the tribe of Simeon was placed in the southern and western portion of the territory of Judah (Josh. 19:1).

LEVI (33:8–11). Jacob had cursed Levi along with Simeon (Gen. 49:5–7), but the people of Levi had redeemed themselves and therefore were chosen to exercise the priestly role over Israel (18:1–8).

This tribe was tested at Massah and at the waters of Meribah through their representatives, Moses and Aaron (Exod. 17:1–7 and Num. 20:1–13), but when Moses came down from Mount Horeb and faced the camp in rebellion (Exod. 32:26), the people of Levi rallied to his side. The result was that the Levites slaughtered three thousand of the worst offenders in order to stop any further judgment on the nation (Exod. 32:27). This tribe was therefore set aside as servants of God. Even though they still could not own any land for an inheritance, they became the spiritual representatives of the nation (Exod. 32:29).

The tribe was charged with three specific duties in ministering before the Lord. First, they would have the Thummim and Urim in their hands. We can only guess the meaning of this, but they were possibly two flatstones kept in the breastplates of the high priests (Exod. 28:30; Lev. 8:8). When the people needed to ascertain the will of God, the priest threw both flatstones onto a flat surface. Each stone had words inscribed on it: Urim on one side and Thummim on the other side. Urim was understood to be no, while Thummim was yes. If both stones came up with Urim on the top side, then the answer was no; but if the stones came up with Thummim, then the answer was yes.

Second, the priests were to be the teachers of the law (33:10a), responsible that each generation should understand the covenant and the rest of the Word of God. If the priests were negligent in their duties, then their failure would condemn them one day when a generation went astray. Third, this tribe also had the care for the worship at the sanctuary, offering the sacrifices as well as burning the incense (33:10b). Moses closed with specific warning to anyone who would dare harm the priests and Levites: God would be their protector and overthrow their foes.

BENJAMIN (33:12). Jacob had described the tribe of Benjamin as people with military prowess (Gen. 49:27), and later on, Deborah mentioned this tribe along with others, who defeated the Canaanites (Judg. 5:14). Moses pictures God's special care for Benjamin. The Lord loved him, perhaps even as Jacob had loved him, and he would dwell in safety under God's special protection.

JOSEPH (33:13–17). In the longest praise of all the tribes, Moses notes two particular blessings, material (33:13–16) and military (33:17). In the latter, there is a poetic description of Joseph, who is represented by the two tribes of Ephraim and Manasseh.

Their land was to be blessed with sufficient dew from heaven, as well as water from beneath (33:13), providing for abundant crops. The mention of the sun and the moon perhaps describe the coming and going of the seasons as they affect various crops in different times of the year (33:14). The territory of Ephraim and Manasseh, which covered a large part of northern Israel, including mountains and hills with a wealth of forests, would be blessed with productivity (33:15). The blessings were climaxed with "the best gifts of the earth and its fullness" (33:16). However, the second line of the verse is puzzling: "The favor of him who dwelt in the burning bush." The language is reminiscent of Moses' encounter with God at the burning bush in the Sinai (Exod. 3:2–4), where God met Israel and the covenant was given. The experience of blessing at the Sinai appears to be the context of further blessings which would rest on the head of Joseph and on the brow of the prince-leader of this tribe. Joseph is the central figure among the

twelve tribes, and the location of the territory given to Ephraim
and Manasseh meant that they controlled a major share of the
northern territory of Israel.

Finally verse 17 pictures Joseph as the Lord's first-born
bull, sacred to the Lord, mighty in battle and used of God to
defeat the enemies of Israel. Even though Judah is a prominent
tribe from whom the Messiah comes, Joseph had the rights of
the first-born (1 Chron. 5:1–2). Joseph's blessings will branch
out to both his sons, but Ephraim will become the dominant
tribe (see also Gen. 48:8–20), designated by the ten thousands,
while Manasseh was described as thousands in number (33:17).

ZEBULUN AND ISSACHAR (33:18–19). The blessings on
these two tribes, Zebulun in their going out and Issachar in the
tents, describe their joy in every area of life (33:18). The first two
lines of verse 19 are difficult to ascertain, but the message
probably refers to the wealth of these two tribes. In the festivals
at the central sanctuary, they will have an abundance to bring;
they will liberally rejoice and thank God for His provisions. One
source of their income was to be in the wealth of the sea,
suggesting seafood and some kind of marine commerce.
Whether this means these tribes will have access to either the
Mediterranean or the Galilee, we are not sure, but both are
possible. The treasures hidden in the sand might mean either
dyes made from shellfish or glass from the sand; perhaps both
are intended.

GAD (33:20–21). Moses' blessings on Gad's "domain"
could be the "broadlands," a territory east of the lower half of
the Jordan River (3:12–16). Gad is pictured as a lion, or lioness,
tearing the arm and head. Perhaps the phrase describes the
tribe's part in the battle for land west of the Jordan, taking the
best part of it, the leader's portion, for itself (33:21). Gad fought
well in the battle, fulfilling what the Lord wanted in conquering
the land.

DAN (33:22). The description of Dan as the lion's cub is a
phrase Jacob already had used to describe Judah (Gen. 49:9).
We are not sure how Dan was associated with Bashan in the
early days, but in a later period, the tribe would conquer
territory in northern Israel (Judg. 18) along with Dan, Naphtali,
and Asher, who also had territory in the north, the Galilee
region (33:23–25).

NAPHTALI (33:23). This tribe was located near the Galilee area, and it was to abound in the favor of the Lord and be full of His blessing. The word, "lake," is the Sea of Galilee, but as to what is meant by "southward to the lake" is unknown.

ASHER (33:24–25). The name "Asher" means "blessed, happy." Asher is described as the favorite of the tribes. The phrase "bathe his feet in oil" may refer to olive trees since they were abundant on the hills of Galilee, or the phrase could be a general term meaning richness or prosperity. Asher's territory also stretched along the coastal area of what is today the distance between Haifa and Tyre. The tribe was on the northern border of Israel, a strategic position for protecting the country. The promise for protection was that the bolts of their gates should be as iron and bronze. In a sense, God gave His word that He would be with Asher should an army attack Israel from the north.

An interesting observation is that the reference to oil is today interpreted as crude oil necessary to run machines of the modern industrial world. There have been many recent explorations for oil in this area of modern Israel, and we can only trust it might be so for Israel's sake.

The concluding hymn of praise (33:26–29) once more describes the Lord God of Jeshurun. Because Israel had been given such a favored name, they were assured that God will be with them in the conquest of the land. The image of God riding on the heavens and on the clouds in His majesty assured His people that He will fight for them. This imagery occurs elsewhere in the Old Testament (Ps. 18:10; 68:33; Isa. 19:1), but it also was well known to the Canaanites. The Lord also reminds Israel that He who is eternal will be the refuge and support for His people and will bear them up as they are faithful to their task (33:27). His battle plan for Israel was to drive out the enemy, destroying them because He had a score to settle with the pagan peoples of the land whose cup of iniquity had more than run over. Never in any case should Israel think that it was by the strength of their hand that they accomplished the task. They were to be the channel for God to work.

When Israel would be faithful and do what God asked of them, they would then be able to live in safety and security

(33:28). The second line is interesting: "Jacob's spring" or fountain would never fail, and their land would be so productive that it would flow with milk and honey. Not only that, but God's dew and rains would be more than adequate to make the land extremely fertile.

Finally, Moses breaks forth into a hymn of praise. He asks rhetorically, who is like Israel, the people who have been chosen and constituted as a nation? No one is like Israel, and only God Himself could have made this possible. He will ever be the shield and helper for Israel, and His sword is their glory. Even though Israel always would be victorious in battle, it will only be by God's help and direction as long as His people are faithful to His word.

## D. Moses' Death (34:1–12)

Moses finished his last task and said his last farewells in the blessings of the tribes. He looked back on a life of victory and triumph, and even though there were occasions and moments of failure, these were only a minor part of a lifetime of grand adventure as Israel's mediator, teacher, and lawgiver and as the confidante of God. In a climactic scene, Moses leaves the plains of Moab on the east bank of the Jordan River and climbs to the top of Mount Nebo as he had been told (3:27; 32:49). The summit was on a ridge opposite Jericho, and the highest peak was Pisgah; the view to the west across the Jordan was excellent. While he did not see the entire land beyond the hills of Gilead on the east and the hills of Judea on the west, he saw what represented the entire Promised Land. The territories he viewed were given in a counter-clockwise movement, from north to south, from Gilead to Dan, Naphtali, Ephraim, Manasseh, the area of Judah as far west as the Mediterranean, the Negev (south), and finally, the entire region from the valley of Jericho, the City of Palms as far as Zoar (34:1–3; Judg. 1:16; 3:12–13). The Lord declared to Moses that the land that he viewed was the land promised to the patriarchs. Israel was now to inherit it through actual possession, but God graciously gave Moses the privilege to view it (34:4).

Could there have been some friends with Moses at his very end? We are not sure whether they were with him at the end or whether they discreetly came shortly afterward. The text declares "He buried him"; whether God actually did it or whether others did it on behalf of God, we cannot say for sure (34:5–6). The information provided is that no one knows where his grave is located, suggesting that there could have been something special in that no human being had any part in it. Jude provides a curious statement that Michael, the archangel, disputed with Satan about the body of Moses (Jude 9), and whether Jude had this information from direct revelation or whether he was referring to some well-known tradition, we are not certain.

Moses died when he was one hundred twenty years old (see 31:2 KJV), and though he was no longer able to go out and come in, meaning that his strength was not like that of a much younger man, his eyes were not weak nor his strength gone, suggesting he still had a lot of vigor and strength. Leading Israel as a strong leader until he was one hundred twenty years old was a feat in itself. The entire nation wept and grieved for him for thirty days, the usual time allotted for such an occasion.

With Moses dead, Joshua, now filled with the spirit of wisdom, took the leadership. The nation recognized that Joshua was Moses' successor and gave their allegiance to him as the regent of the Lord the God of Israel (34:9).

The last three verses stress Moses' ministry and the kind of person he was. He was the greatest prophet Israel ever had (18:15–22; Num. 12:6–8). The Lord knew and spoke with him face to face. He was partner to great, miraculous signs and wonders which God performed in order to release Israel from Egypt. He was God's chosen leader to transform a nation of slaves into a free people. In a sense, he had the offices of prophet, priest, and judge. To this day Jewish people everywhere regard him as "Moses our teacher!"

## For Further Study

1. Examine the commentaries to decide whether chapters 29 and 30 should be attached to chapters 31–34 as a unit or whether they should be treated as a single unit in themselves.

2. Compare the Middle Eastern treaties' instructions for reading the covenant with Deuteronomy's instructions for reading the law covenant.

3. Compare the *riv* or legal suit pattern of Moses' song with the similar pattern in the Middle Eastern treaties.

4. Do a word study on the attributes of God in Moses' song.

5. Compare Moses' blessing of the tribes with Jacob's blessings of his sons in Genesis 49. Explain any similarities or differences.

6. Study how the high priest determined the will of God using the Urim and Thummim.

7. Use commentaries to study the leadership roles of the tribe of Joseph (Ephraim and Manasseh) and Judah.

8. Research Jude's information about Michael disputing with Satan over the body of Moses.

# Bibliography

## Commentaries on Deuteronomy

Archer, Gleason L. *A Survey of Old Testament Introduction*. Chicago: Moody Press, 1964.

Craigie, Peter C. *Deuteronomy* in *The New International Commentary on the Old Testament*. Grand Rapids: Wm. B. Eerdmans Publishing Company, 1976.

Driver, S. R. *Deuteronomy* in *The International Critical Commentary*. *3rd ed.* Edinburgh: T. & T. Clark, 1902.

Harper, Andrew. *The Book of Deuteronomy* in *The Expositor's Bible*. New York: Armstrong, 1903.

Keil, C. F. and Delitzsch, F. *The Pentateuch*, Vol. III in *Biblical Commentary on the Old Testament*. Translated by James Martin. Grand Rapids: Wm. B. Eerdmans Publishing Company, 1951.

Kline, Meredith G. *The Structure of Biblical Authority*. Grand Rapids: Wm. B. Eerdmans Publishing Company, 1972.

_____. *Treaty of the Great King*. Grand Rapids: Wm. B. Eerdmans Publishing Company, 1965.

Manley, G. T. *The Book of the Law: Studies in the Date of Deuteronomy*. Grand Rapids: Wm. B. Eerdmans Publishing Company, 1957.

Mayes, A. D. H. *Deuteronomy* in *The New Century Bible Commentary*. Edited by R. E. Clements and M. Black. Grand Rapids: Wm. B. Eerdmans Publishing Company, 1979.

Mendenhall, G. E. "Ancient Oriental and Biblical Law," *The Biblical Archaeologist* XVII (May, 1954).

_____. "Covenant Forms in Israelite Tradition," *The Biblical Archaeologist* XVII(Sept., 1954).

Nicholson, E. W., *Deuteronomy and Tradition*. Philadelphia: Fortress Press, 1967.

Phillips, Anthony. *Deuteronomy* in *The Cambridge Bible Commentary*. Cambridge: University Press, 1973.

von Rad, Gerhard. *Deuteronomy*. Translated by Dorothea Barton. Philadelphia: Westminster Press, 1966.

Segal, M. H. "The Composition of the Pentateuch—A Fresh Examination," *Scripta Hierosolymitana*, Vol. 8, ed. C. Rabin. Jerusalem: Hebrew University, The Magnes Press, 1961.

Thompson, J. A. *Deuteronomy* in *The Tyndale Old Testament Commentaries*. Edited by D. J. Wise. Downers Grove, IL: InterVarsity Press, 1974.

Young, E. J. *An Introduction to the Old Testament*, rev. ed. Grand Rapids: Wm. B. Eerdmans Publishing Company, 1960.

## Collateral Materials Used for the Commentary on Deuteronomy

Aharoni, Y. and Avi-Yonah, M. *The Macmillan Bible Atlas*. New York: The Macmillan Company, 1968.

Danby, Herbert. *The Mishnah, Makkot*. London: Oxford University Press, 1933.

Gesenius, William. *Hebrew and Chaldee Lexicon*. Edited by S. Tregelles. Grand Rapids: Wm. B. Eerdmans Publishing Company, 1950.

Glueck, Nelson. *The Other Side of the Jordan*. New Haven: American Schools of Oriental Research, 1940.

Harrison, R. K. *Introduction to Old Testament*. Grand Rapids: Wm. B. Eerdmans Publishing Company, 1969.

Kaufman, Stephen A. "The Structure of the Deuteronomic Law," MAARAV (1978–79).

Kidner, Derek. "The Origins of Israel," *The Student Fellowship Bulletin*, 57. Inter-Varsity Christian Fellowship, 1970.

Kitchen, K. A. *Ancient Orient and Old Testament*. Downers Grove, IL: InterVarsity Press, 1966.

_____. "Ancient Orient 'Deuteronomism' and the Old Testament," in *New Perspectives on the Old Testament*. Edited by J. Barton Payne. San Diego: Harcourt, 1970.

McCarthy, D. J. *Treaty and Covenant*. Rome: Pontifical Biblical Institute, 1963.

Schaff, Philip. *History of the Christian Church*, Vol. III. Grand Rapids: Wm. B. Eerdmans Publishing Company, 1950.

Weinfeld, M. *Deuteronomy and the Deuteronomic School*. Oxford: Clarendon Press, 1972.